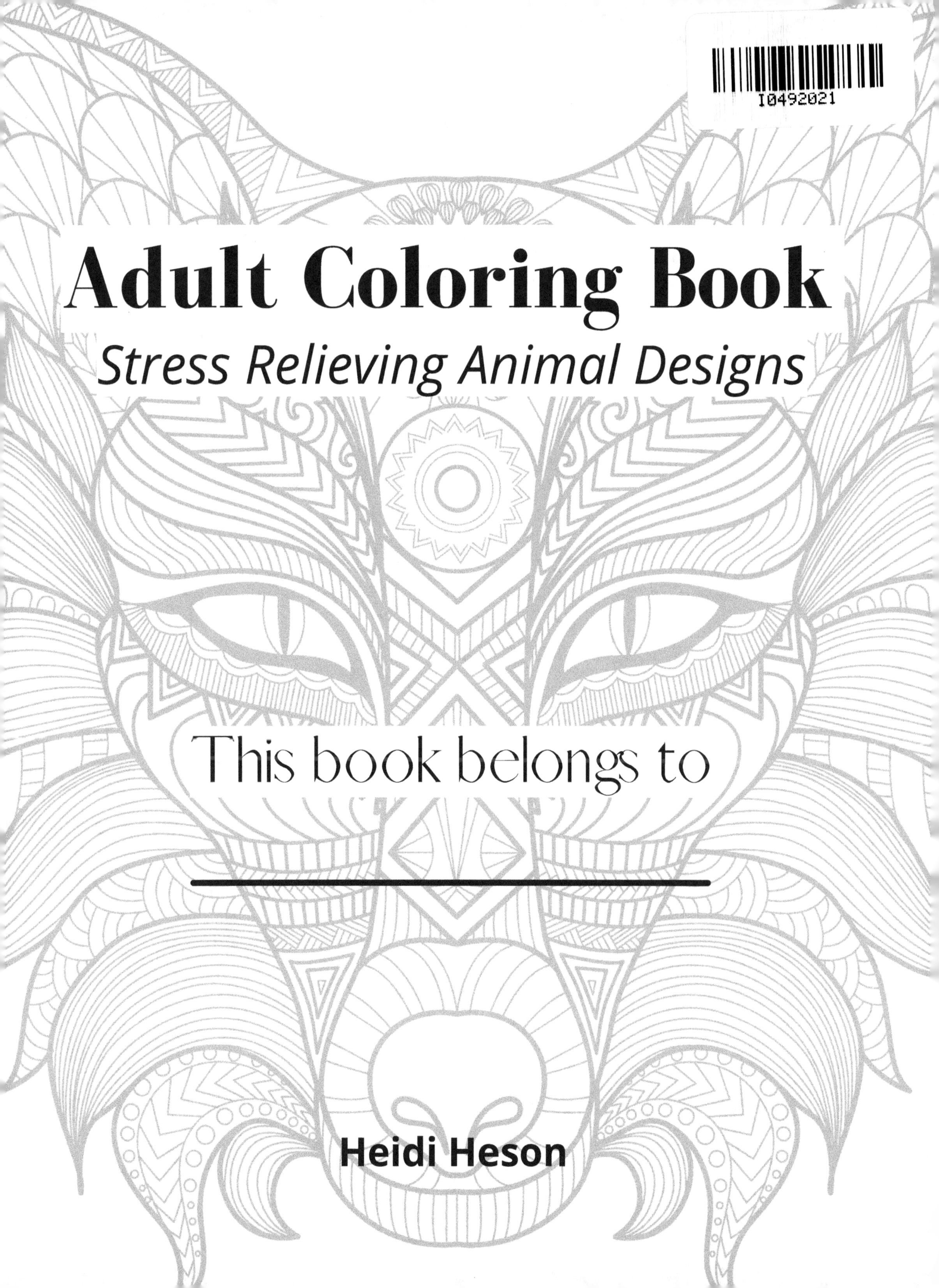

Adult Coloring Book

Stress Relieving Animal Designs

This book belongs to

____

Heidi Heson

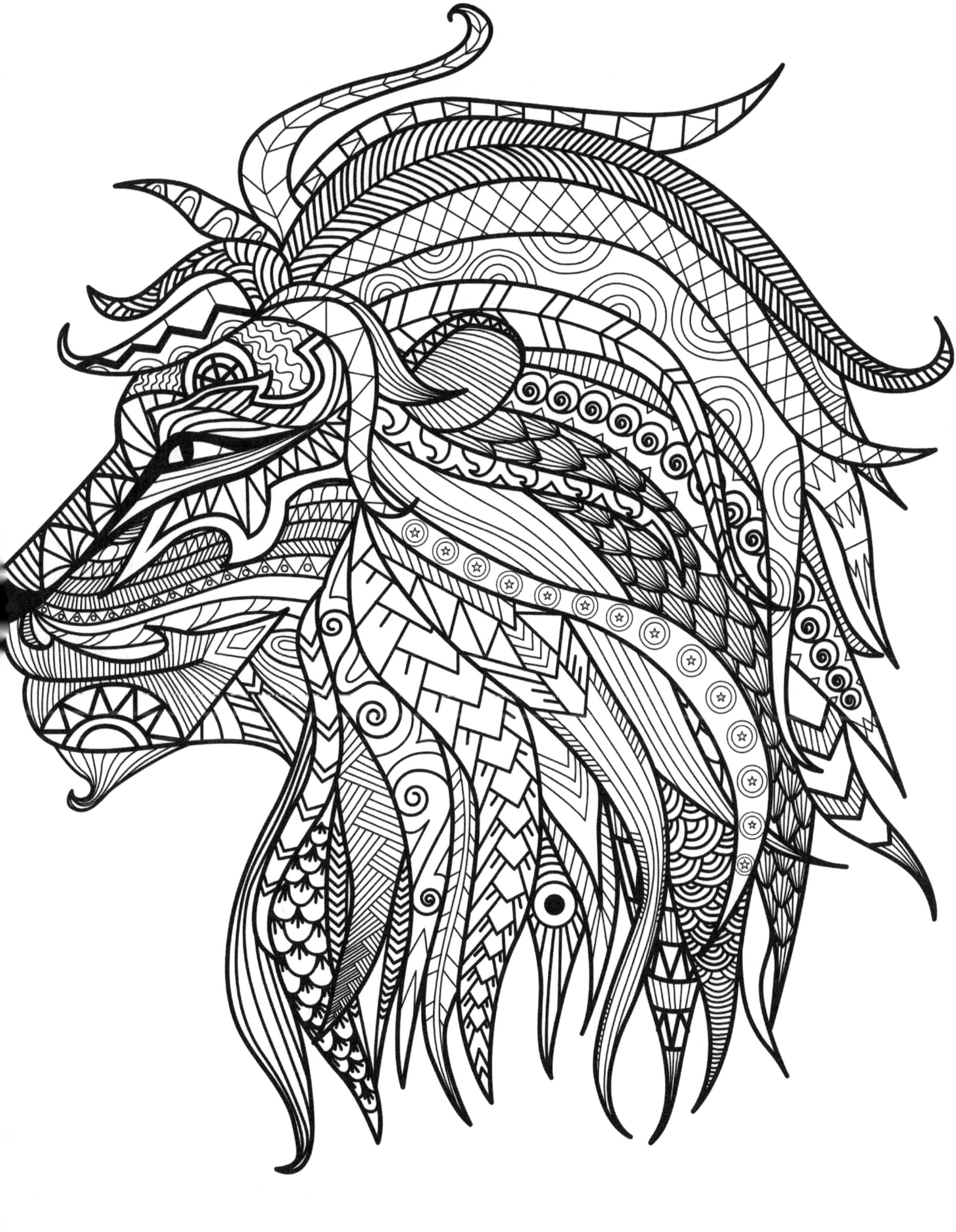

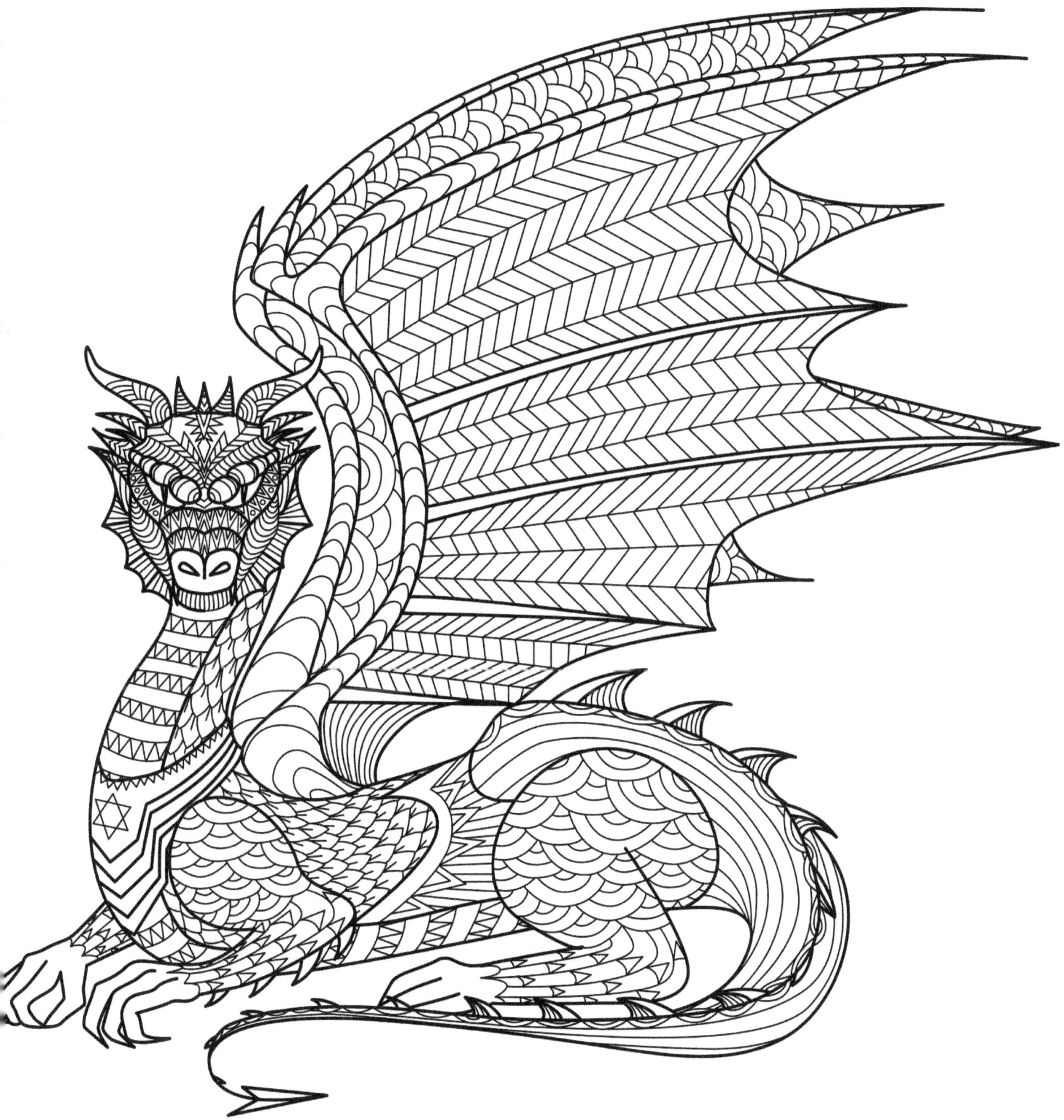

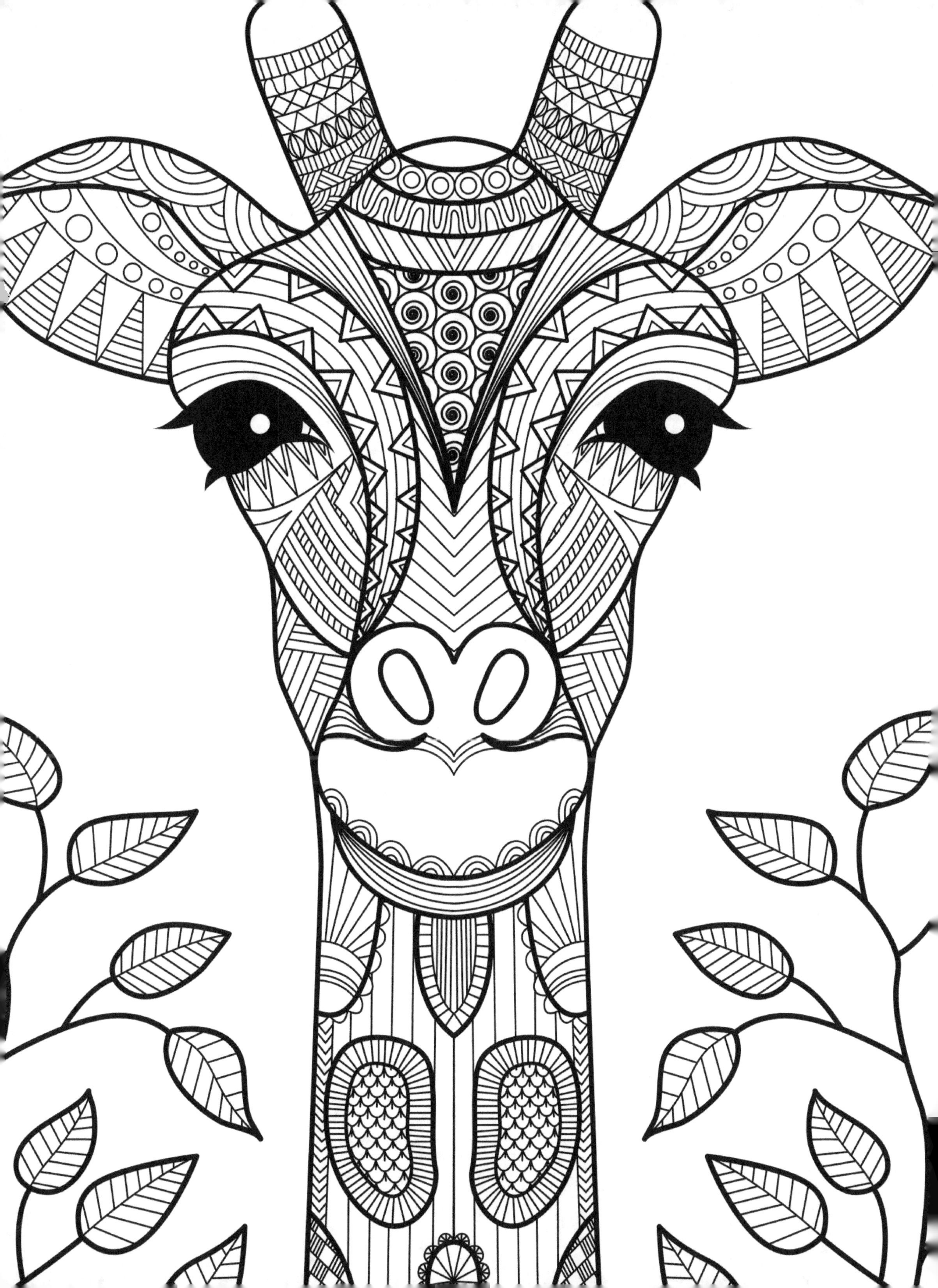

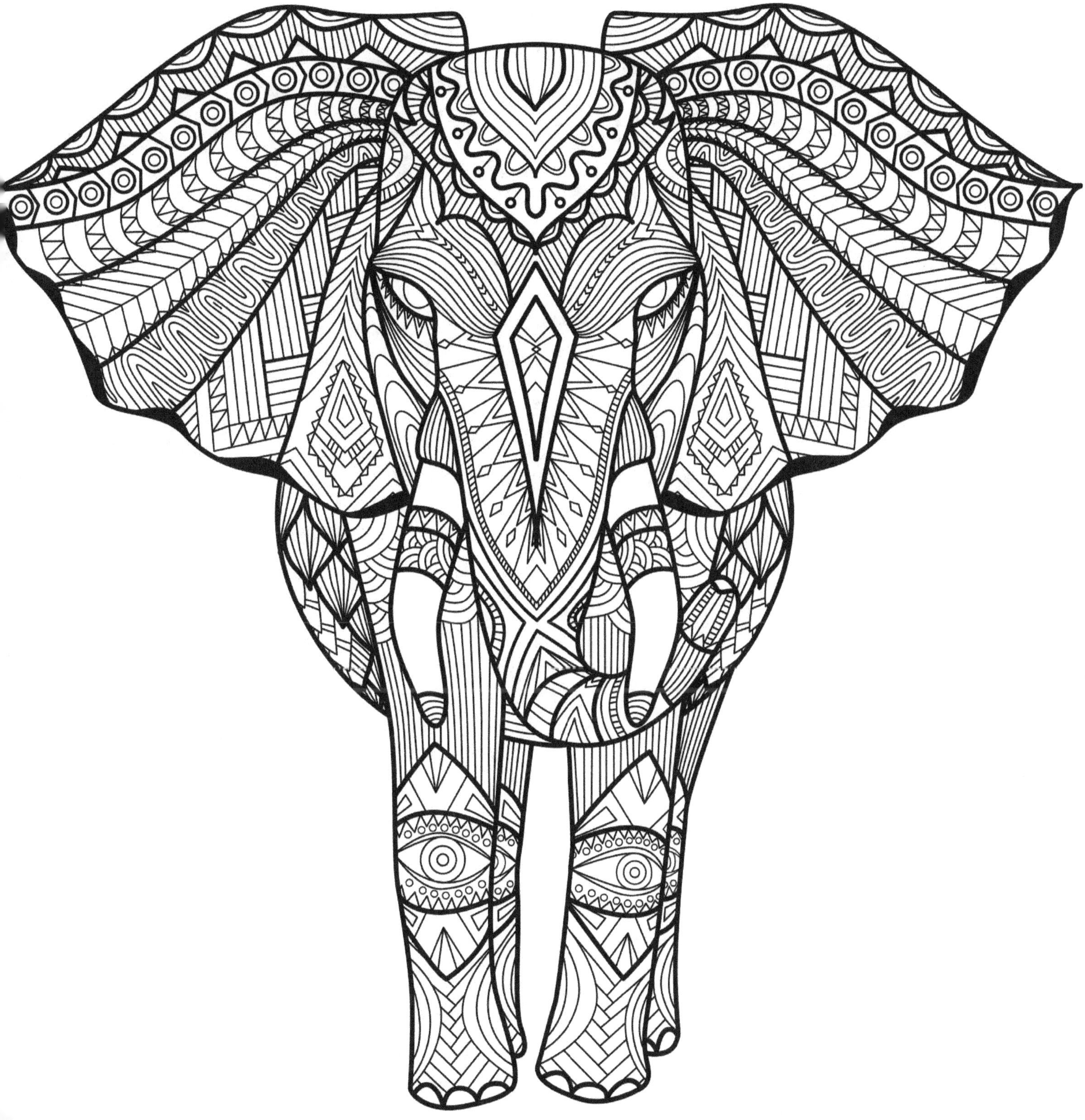

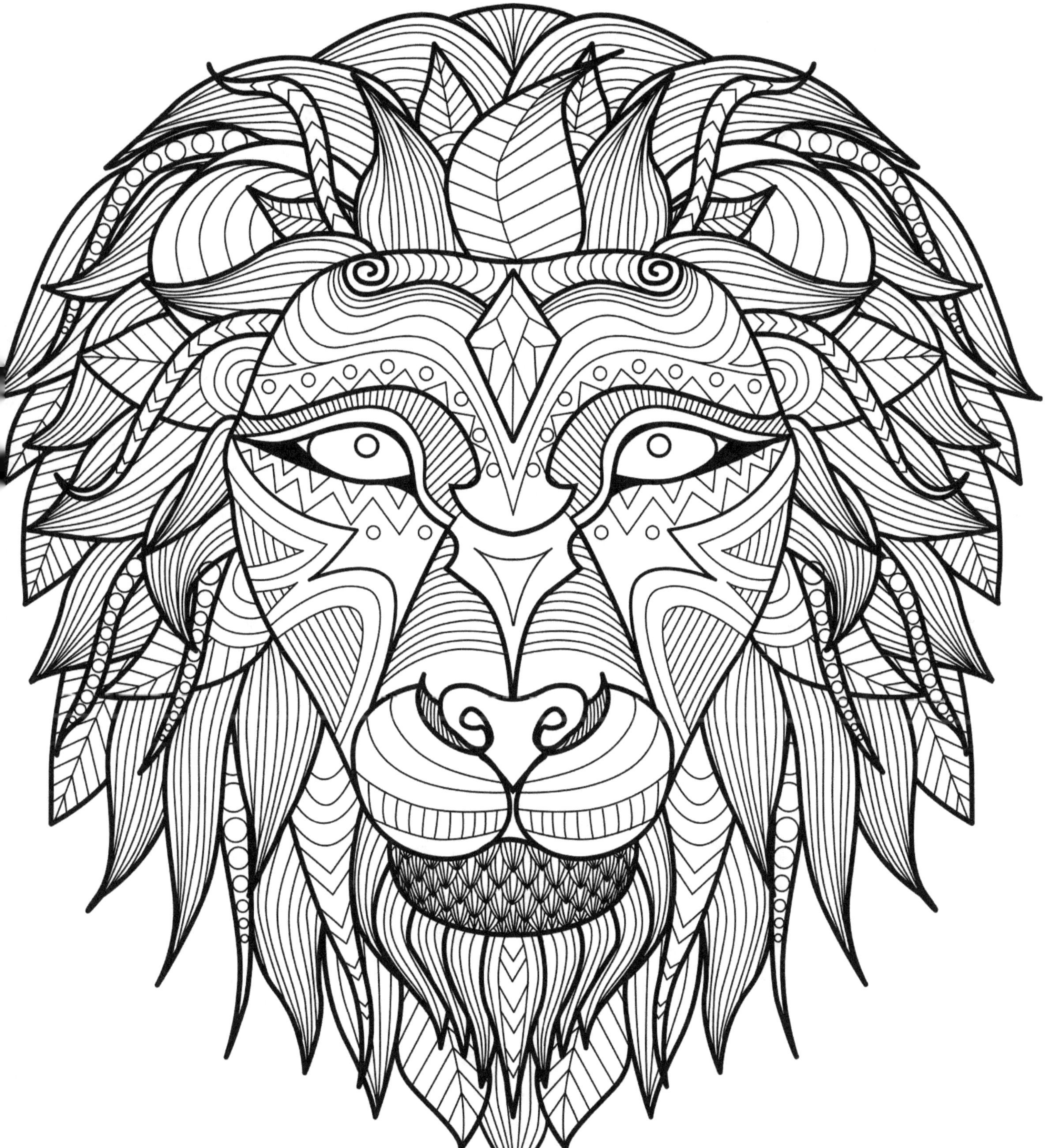

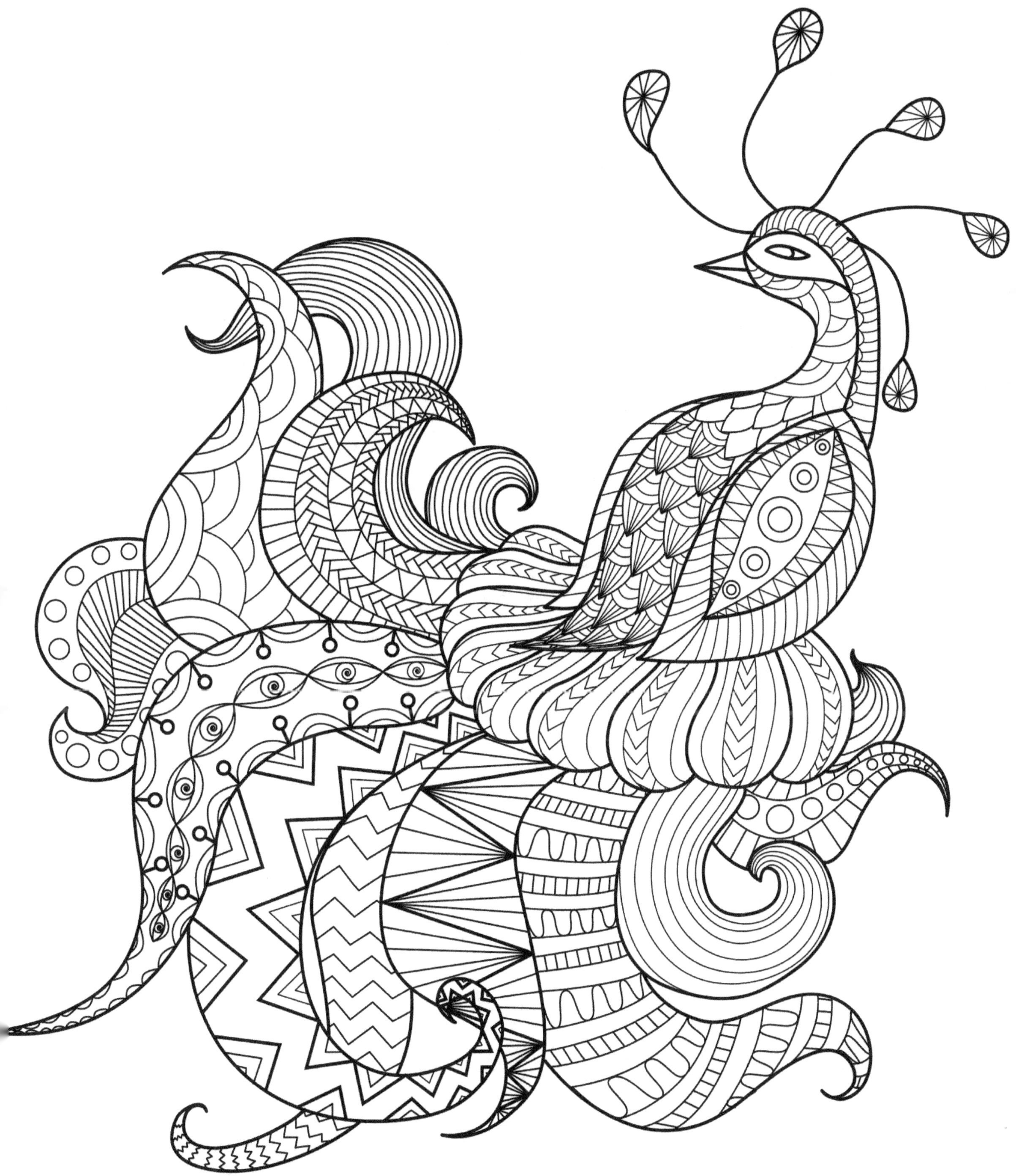

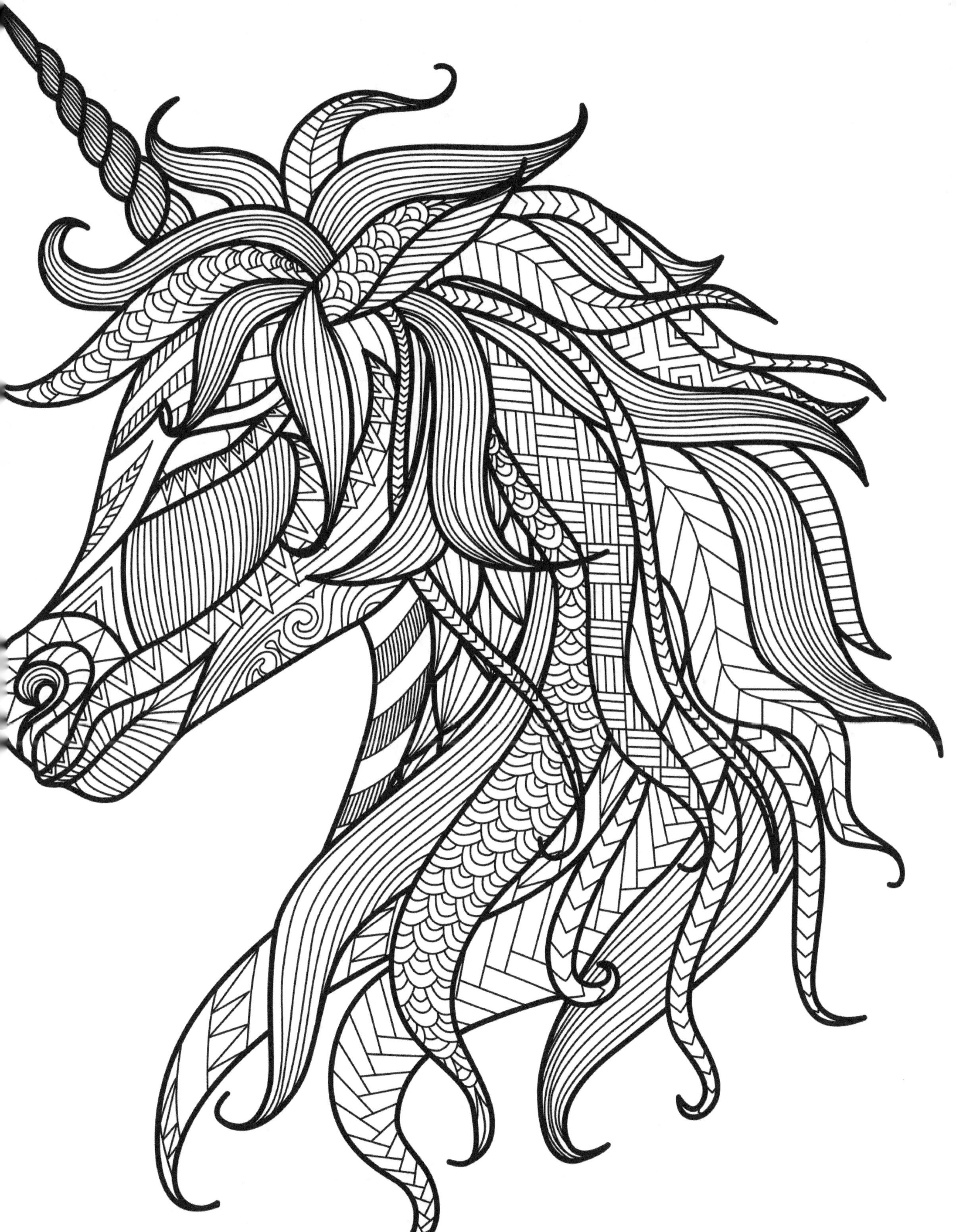

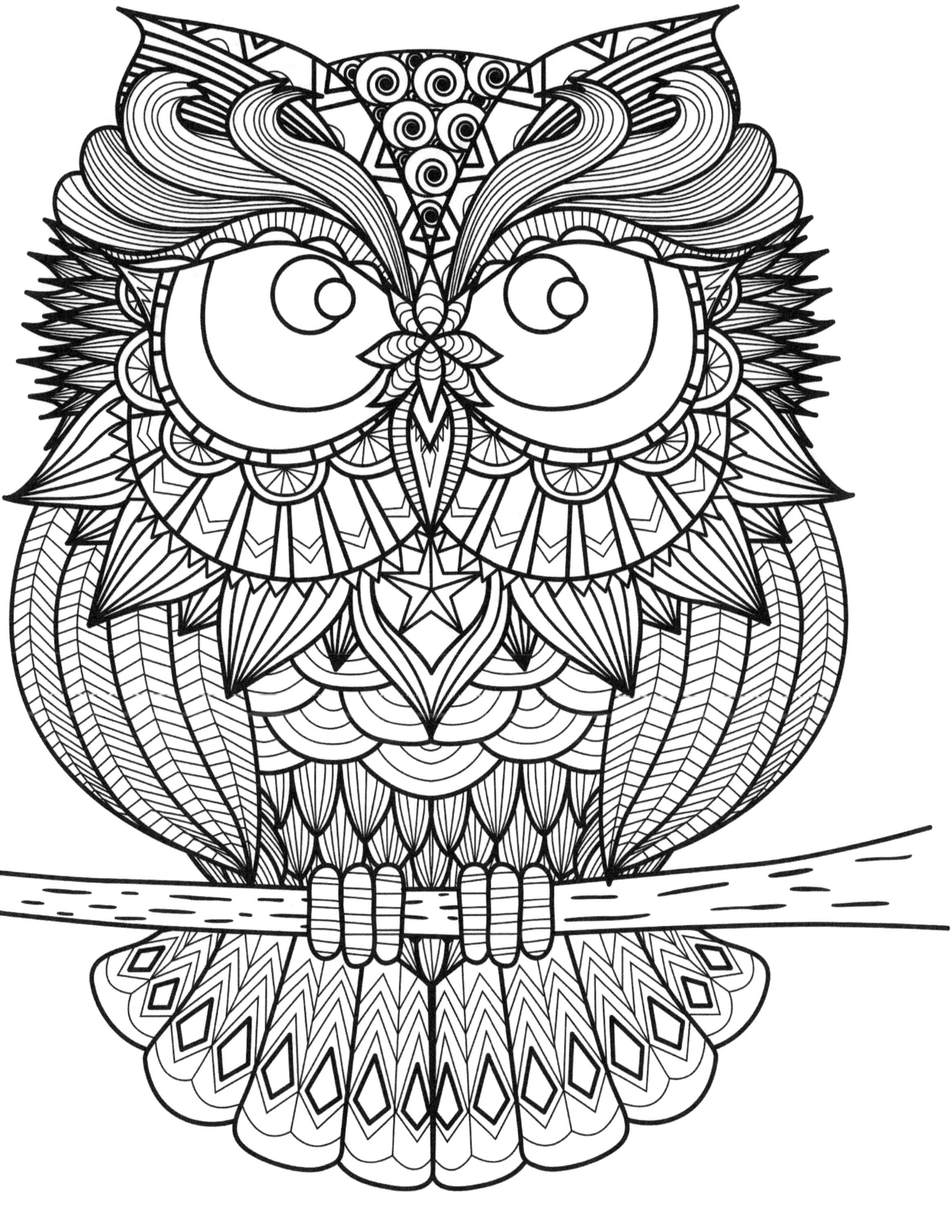

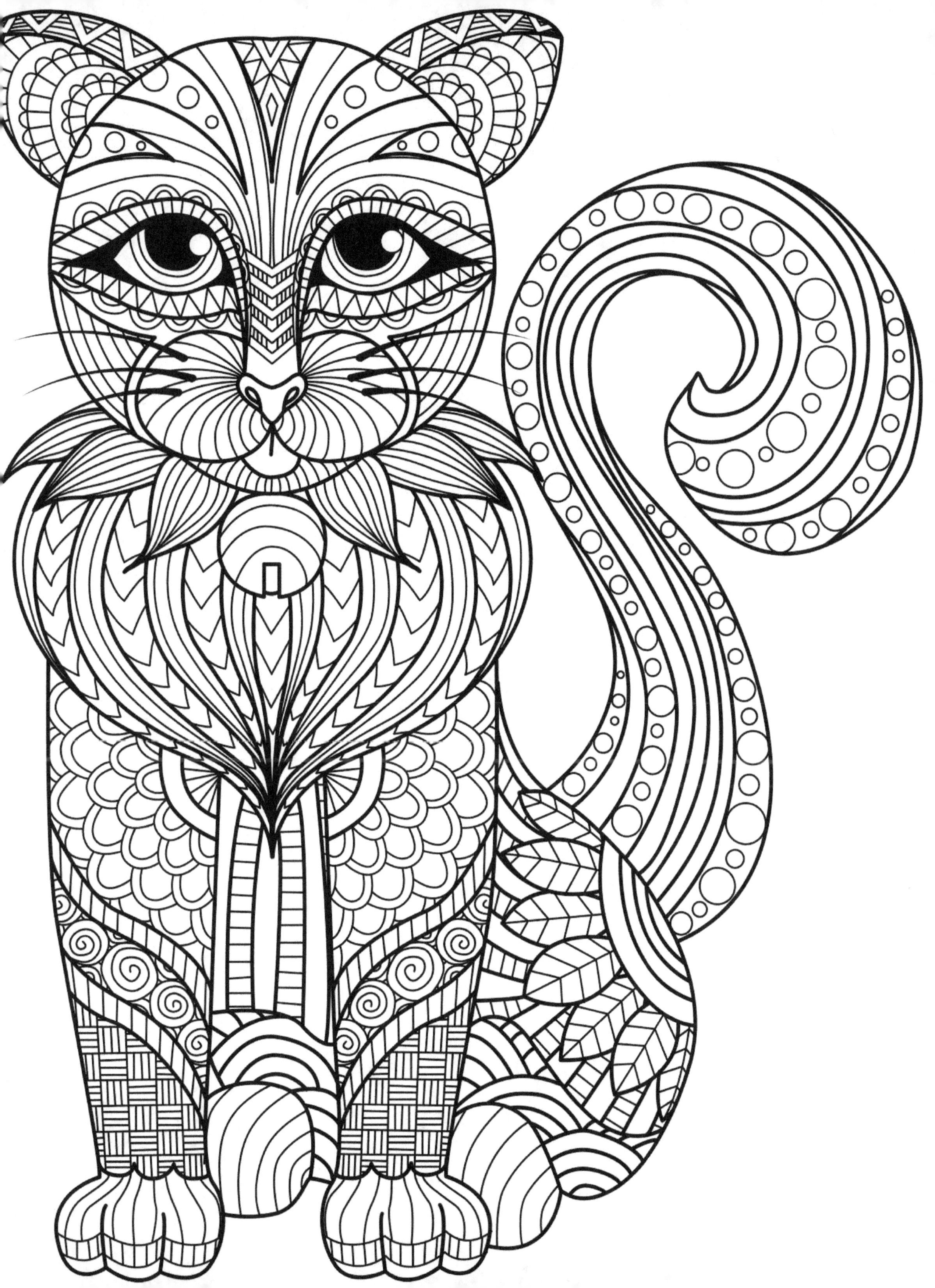

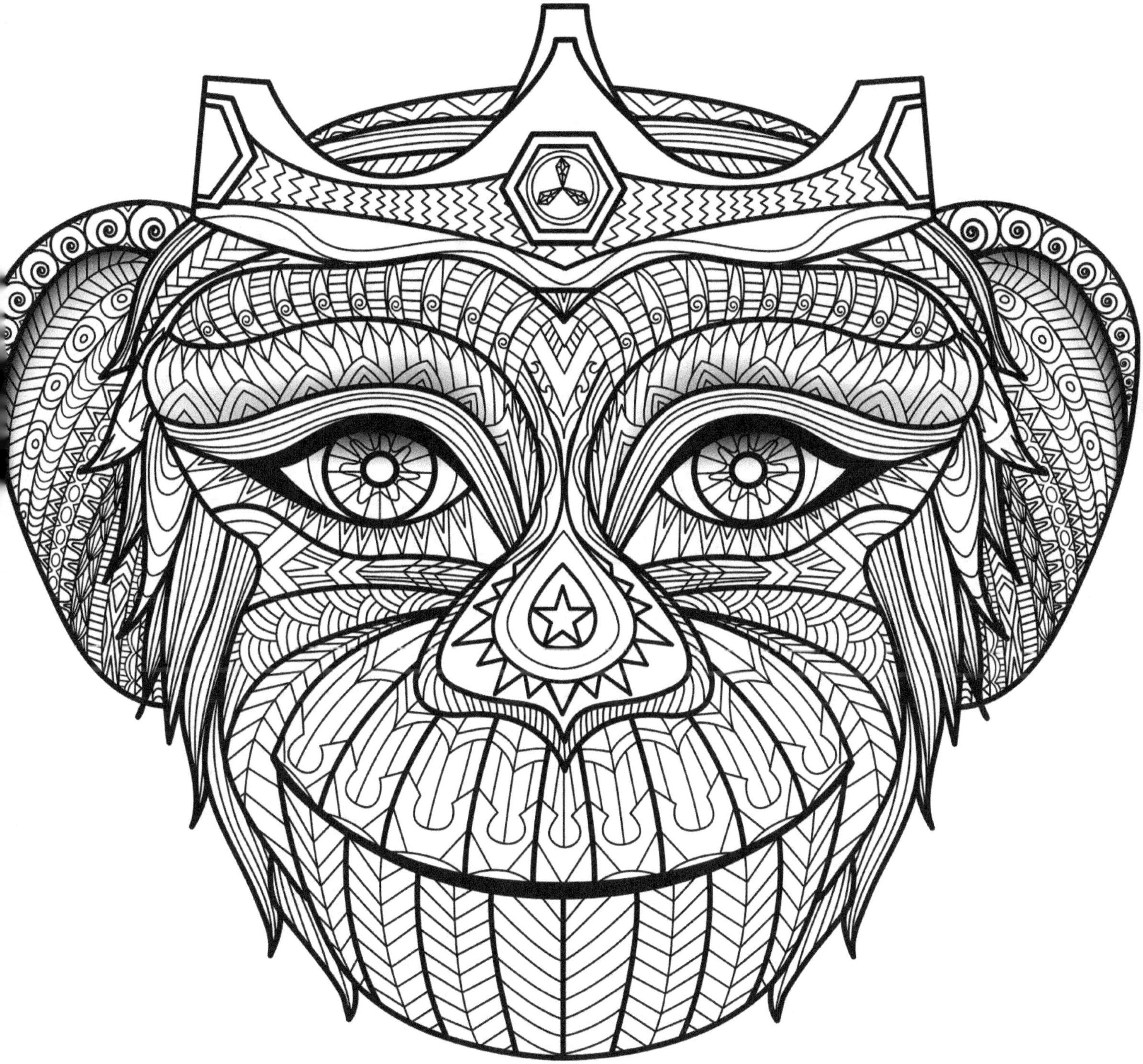

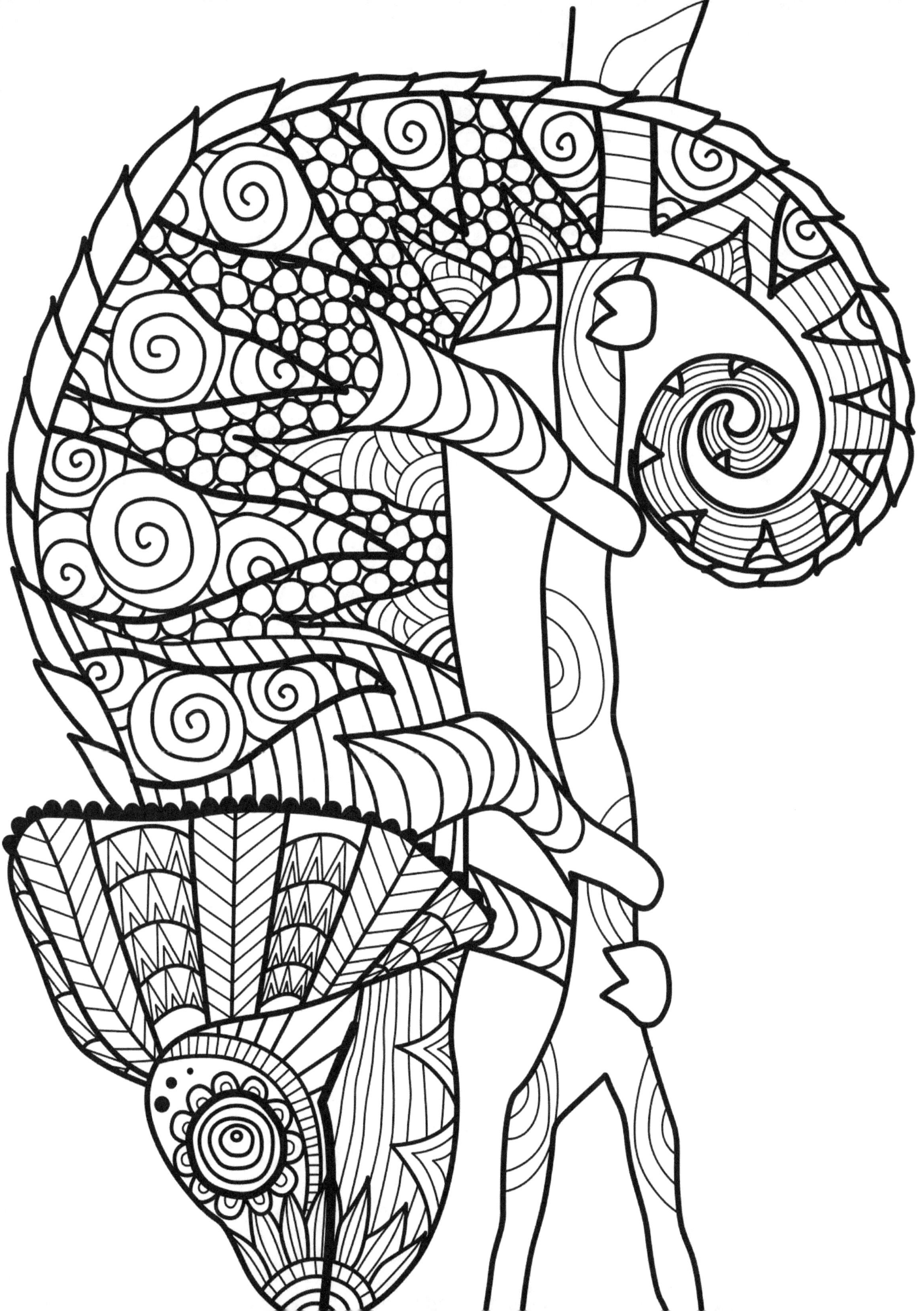

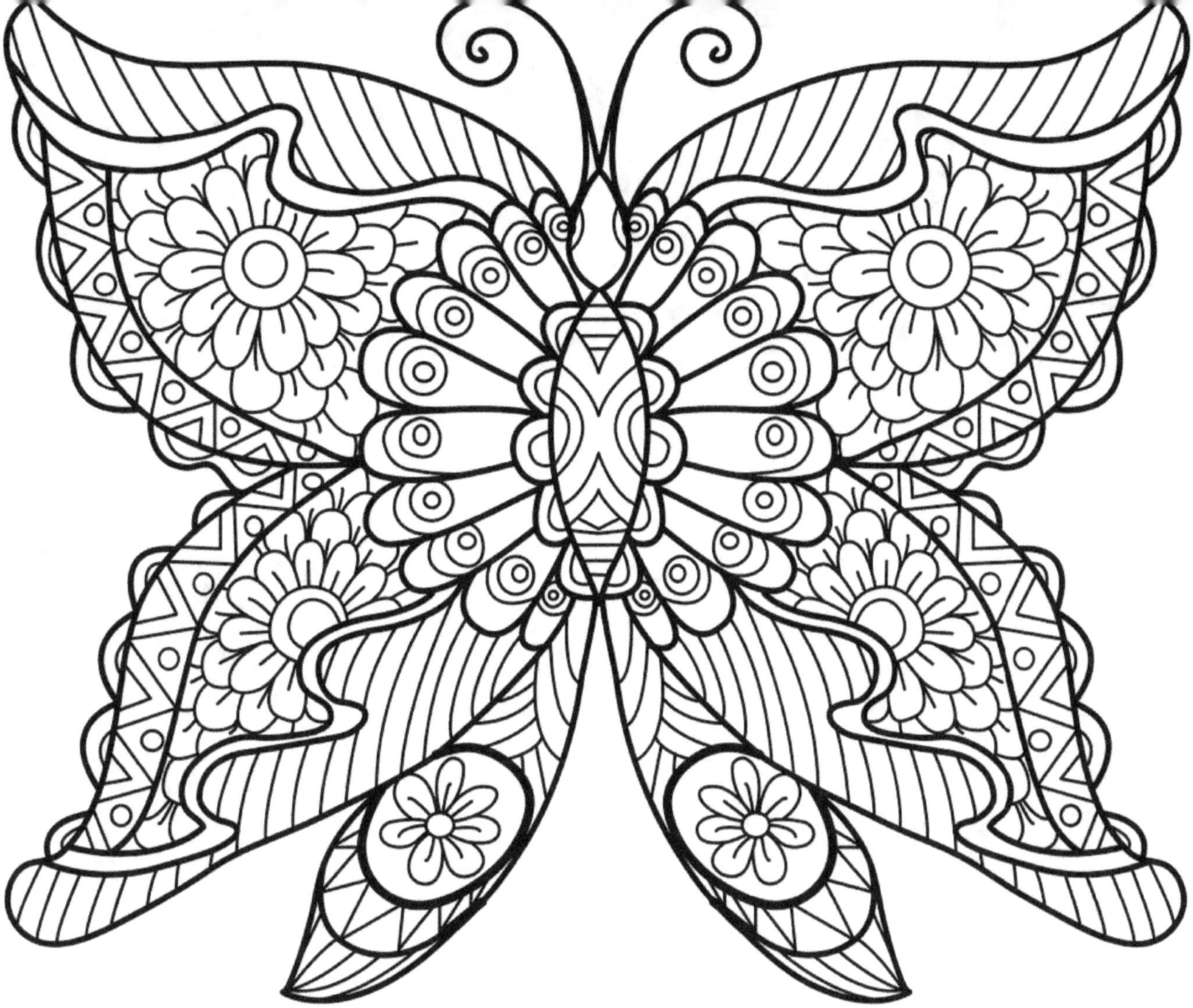

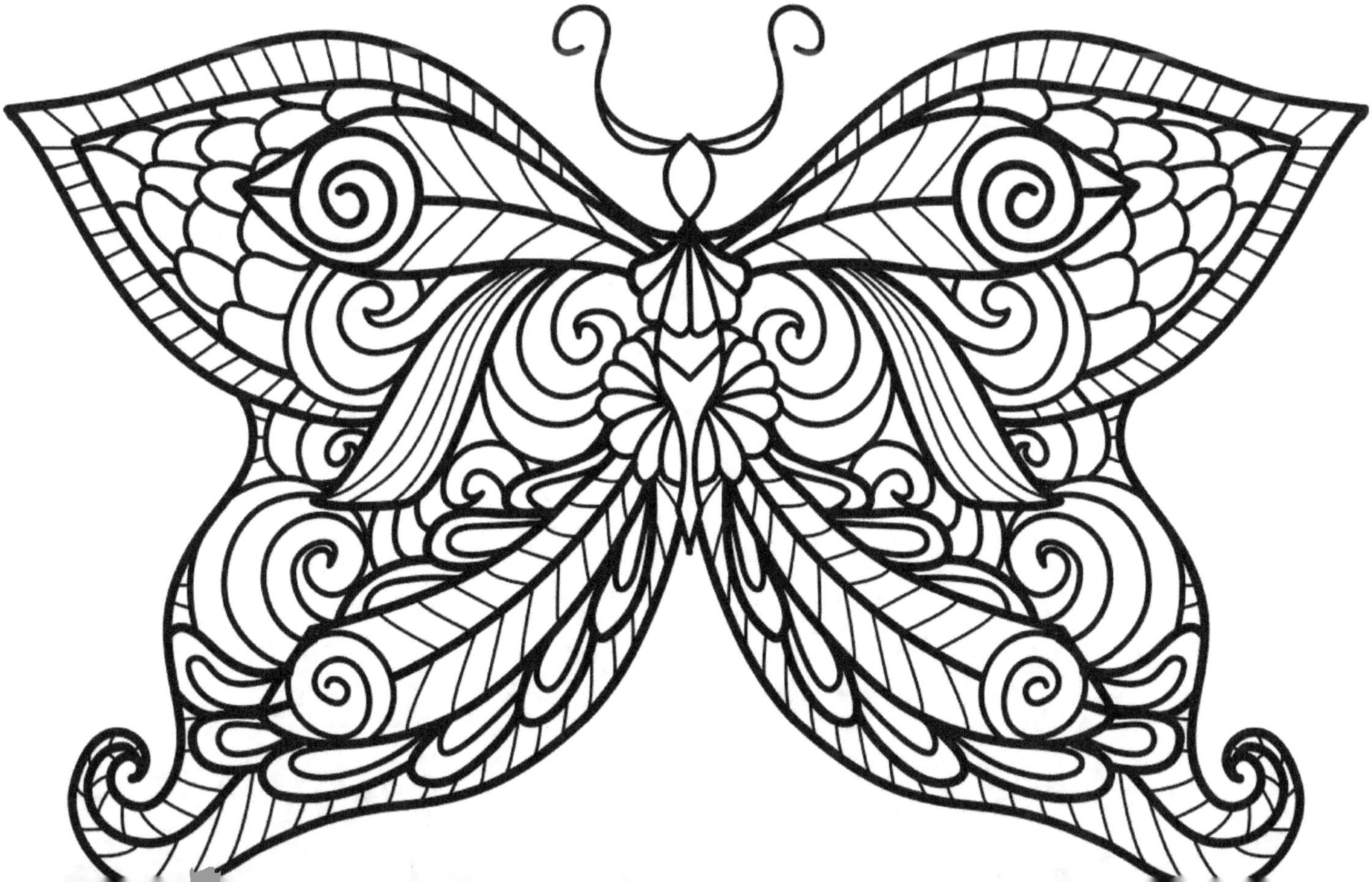

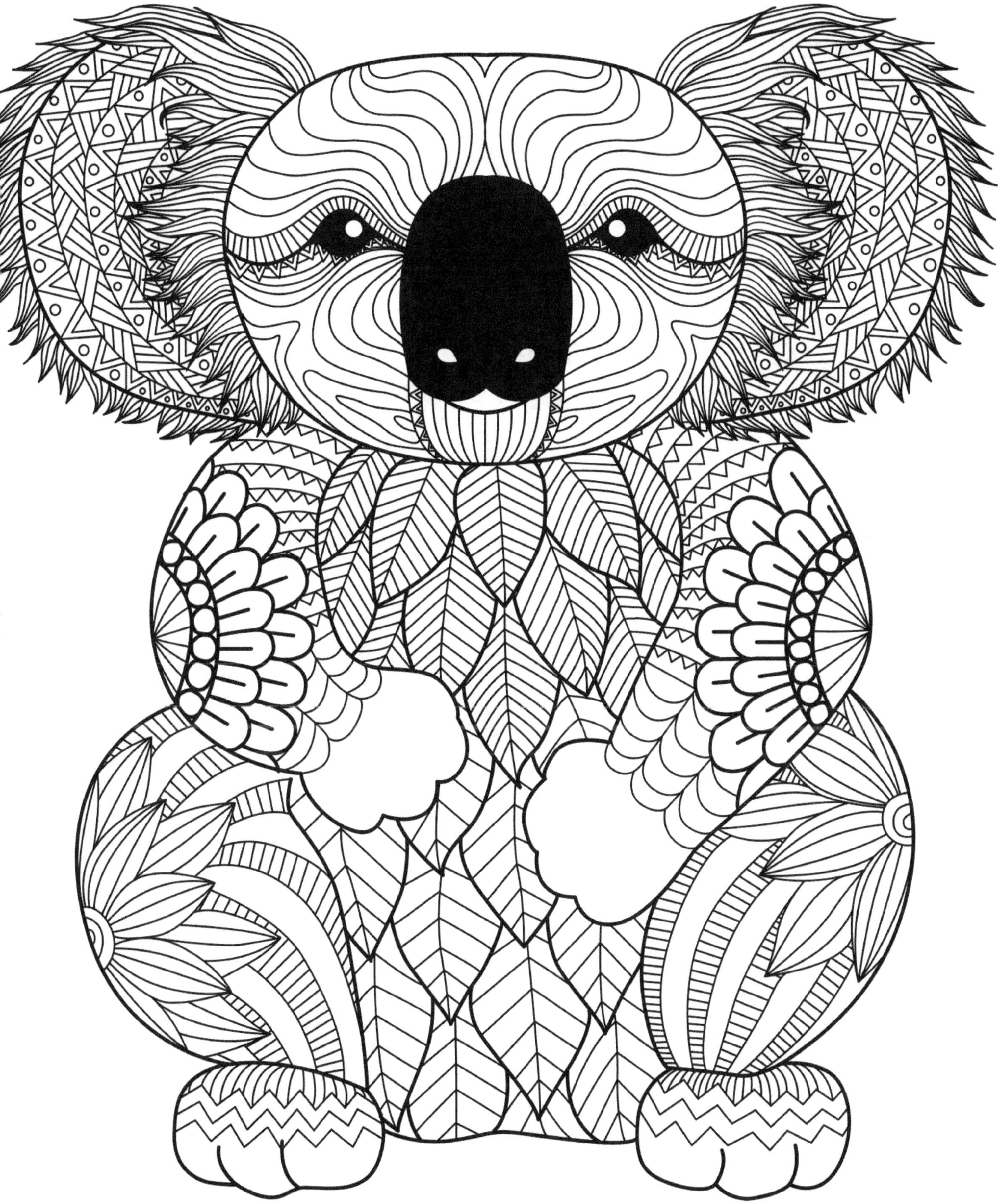

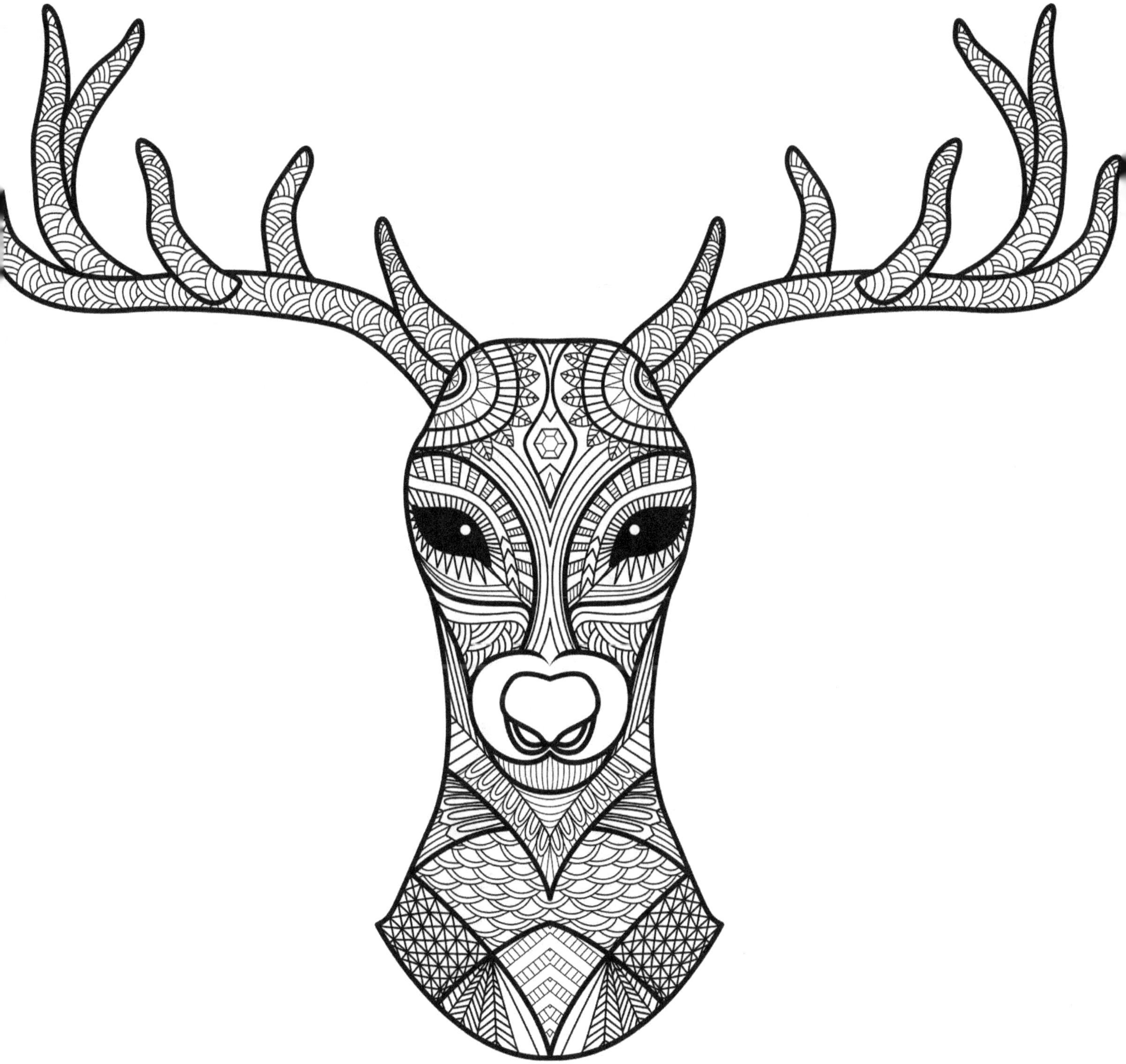

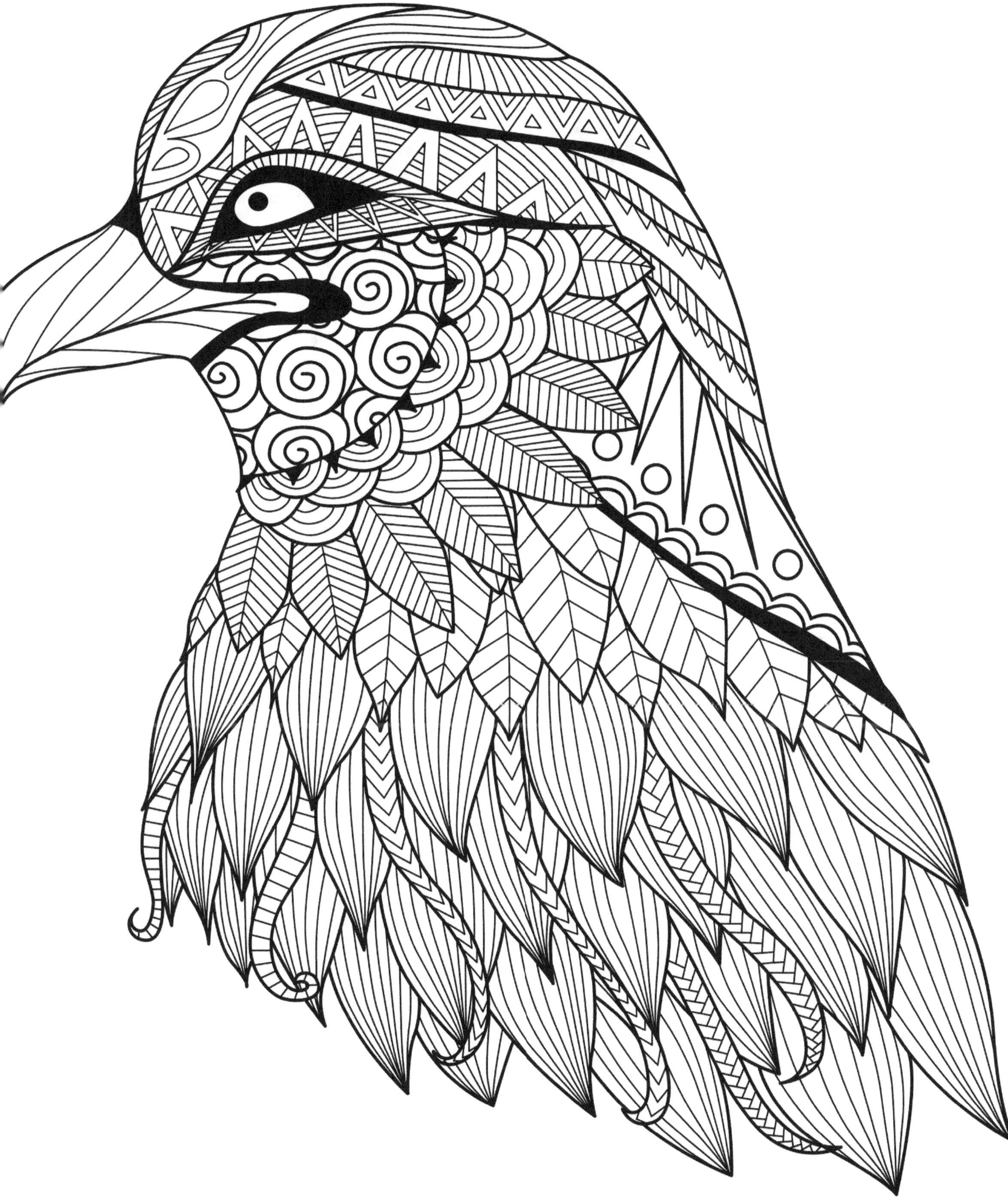

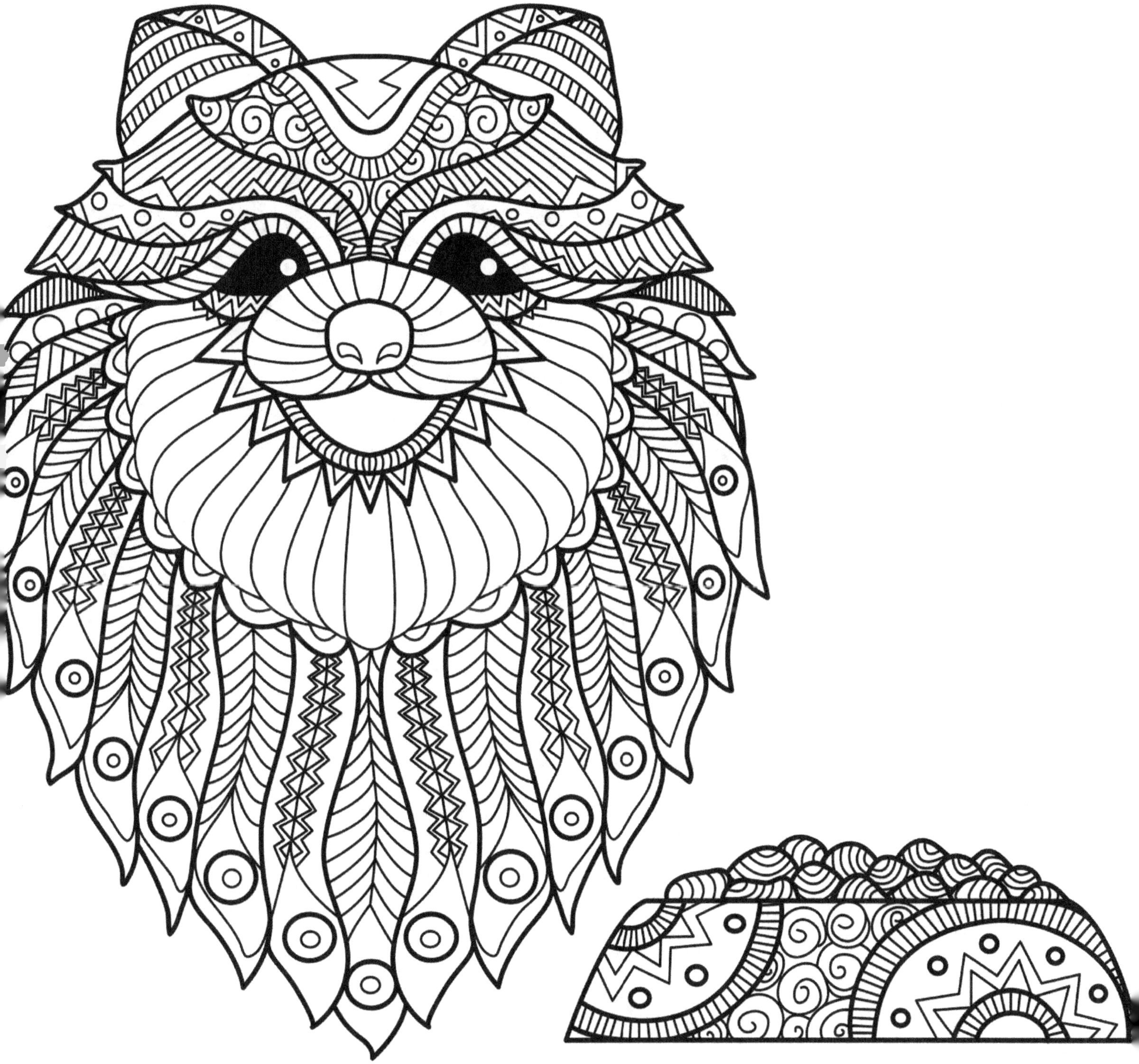

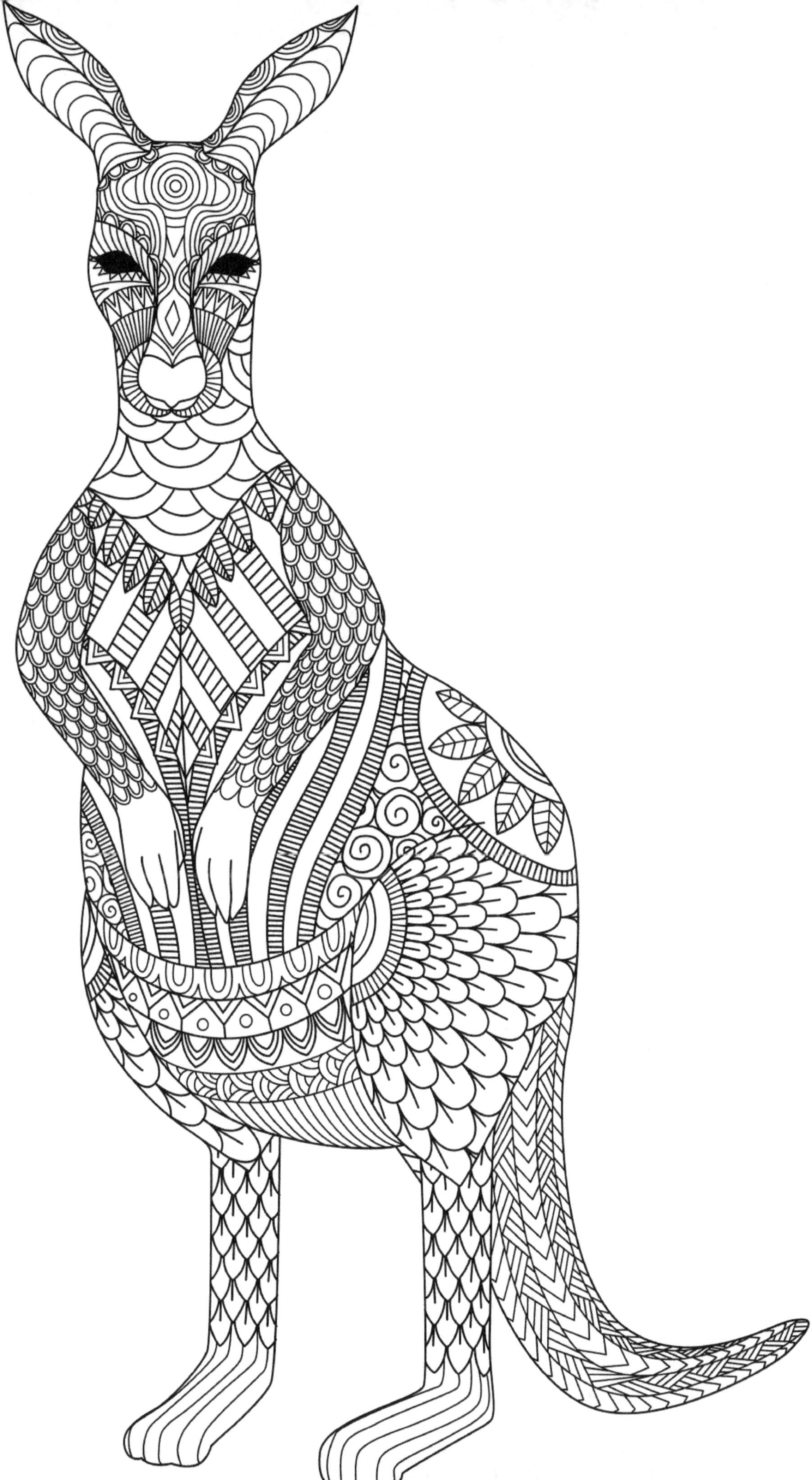

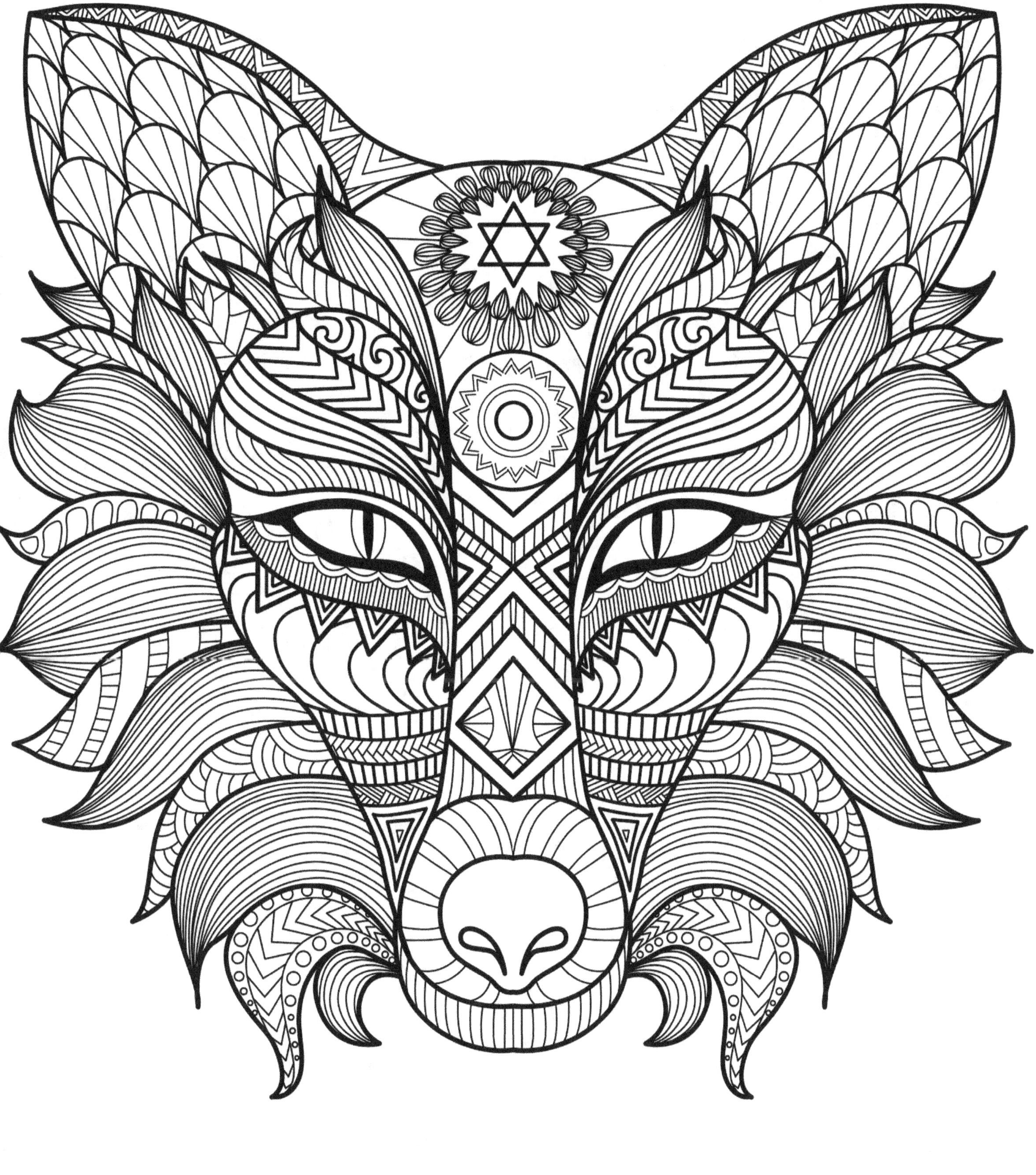

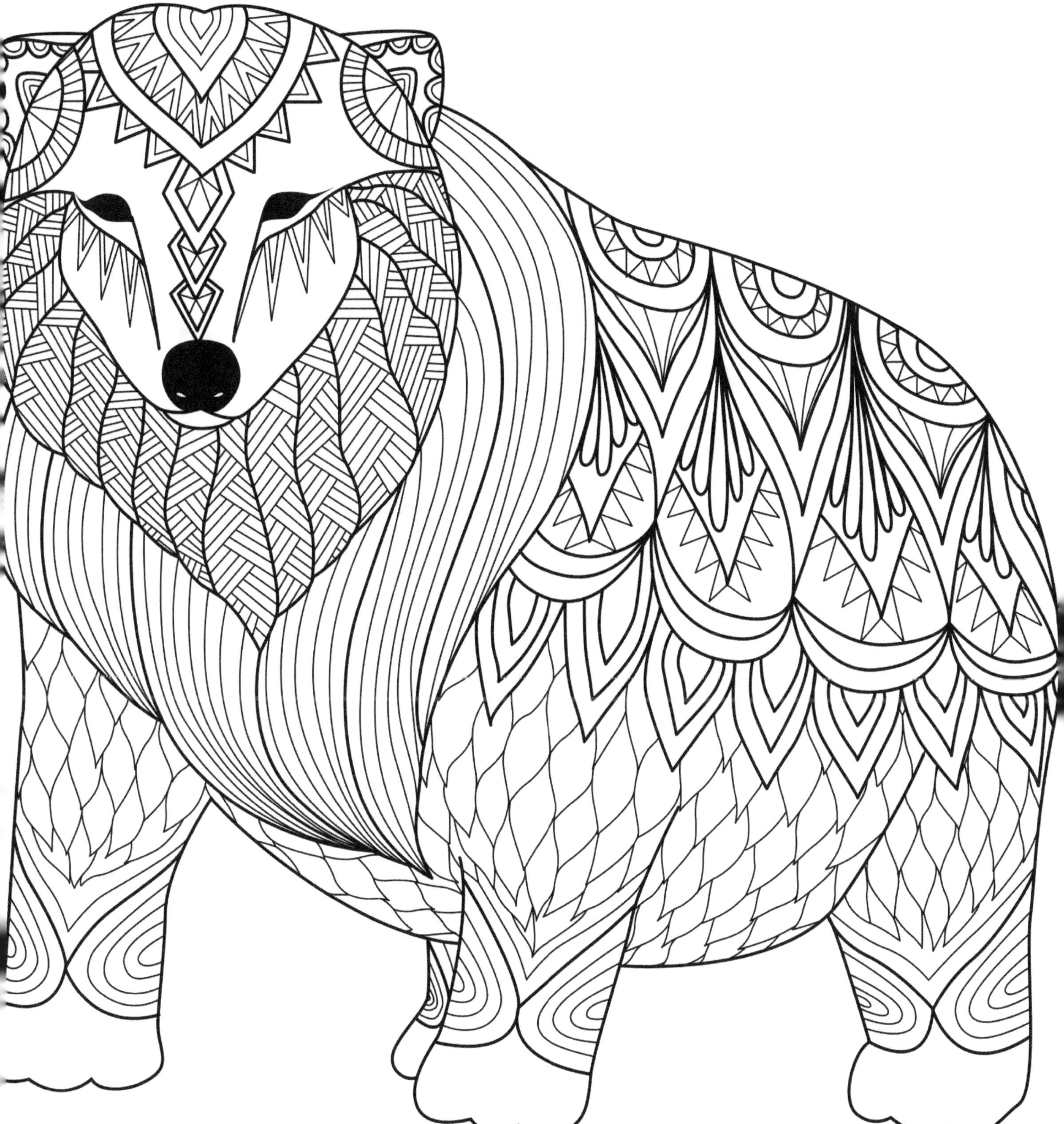

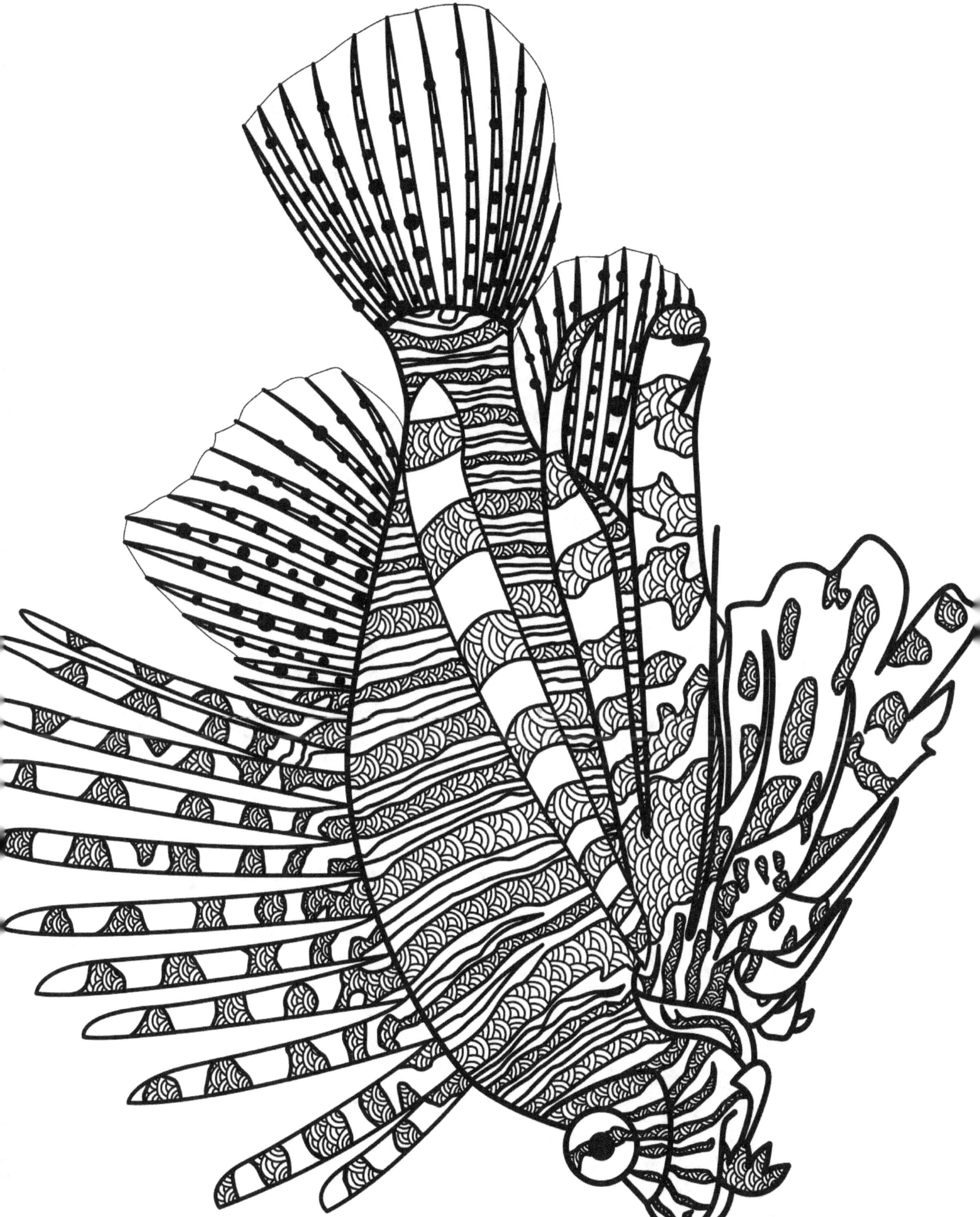

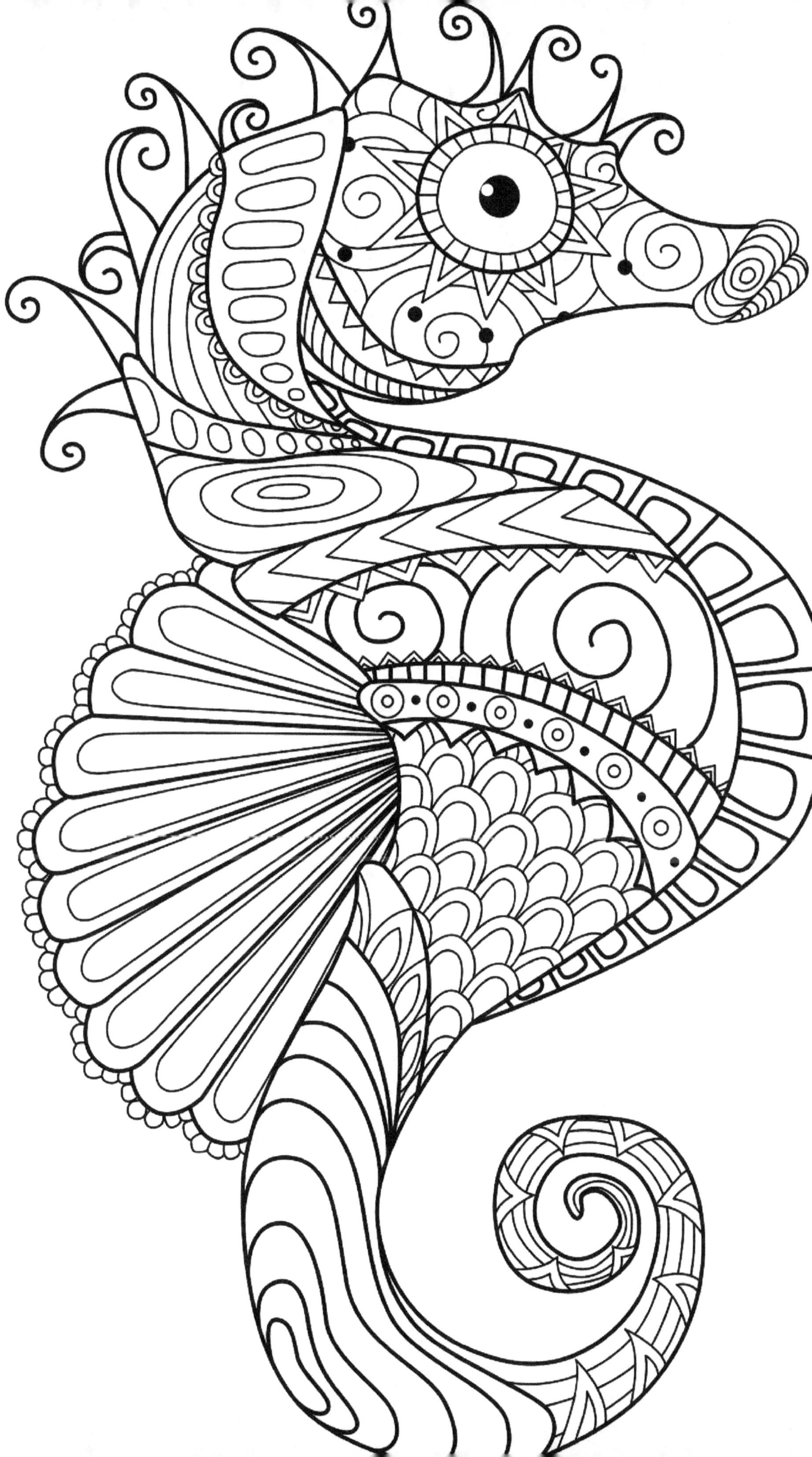

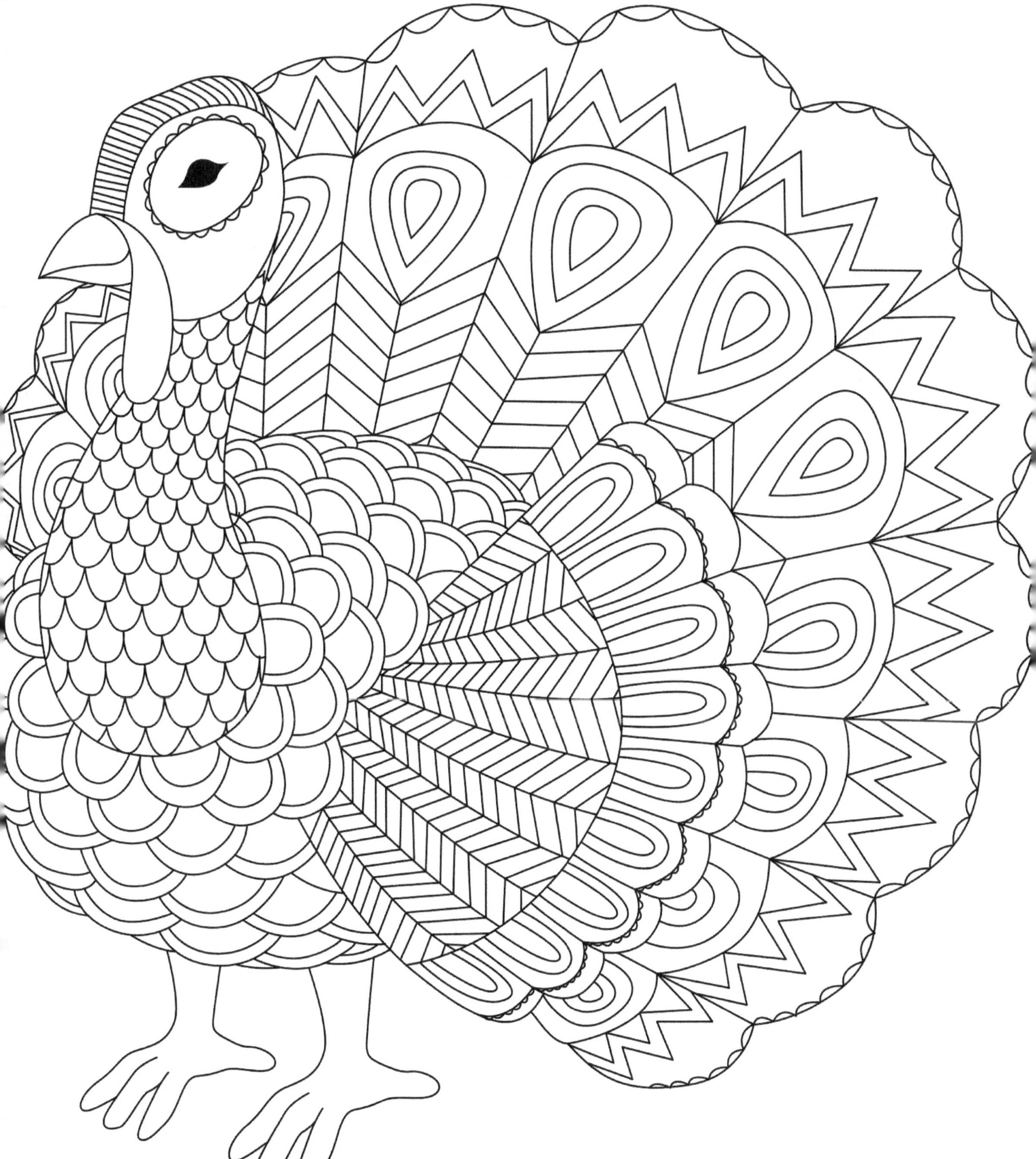

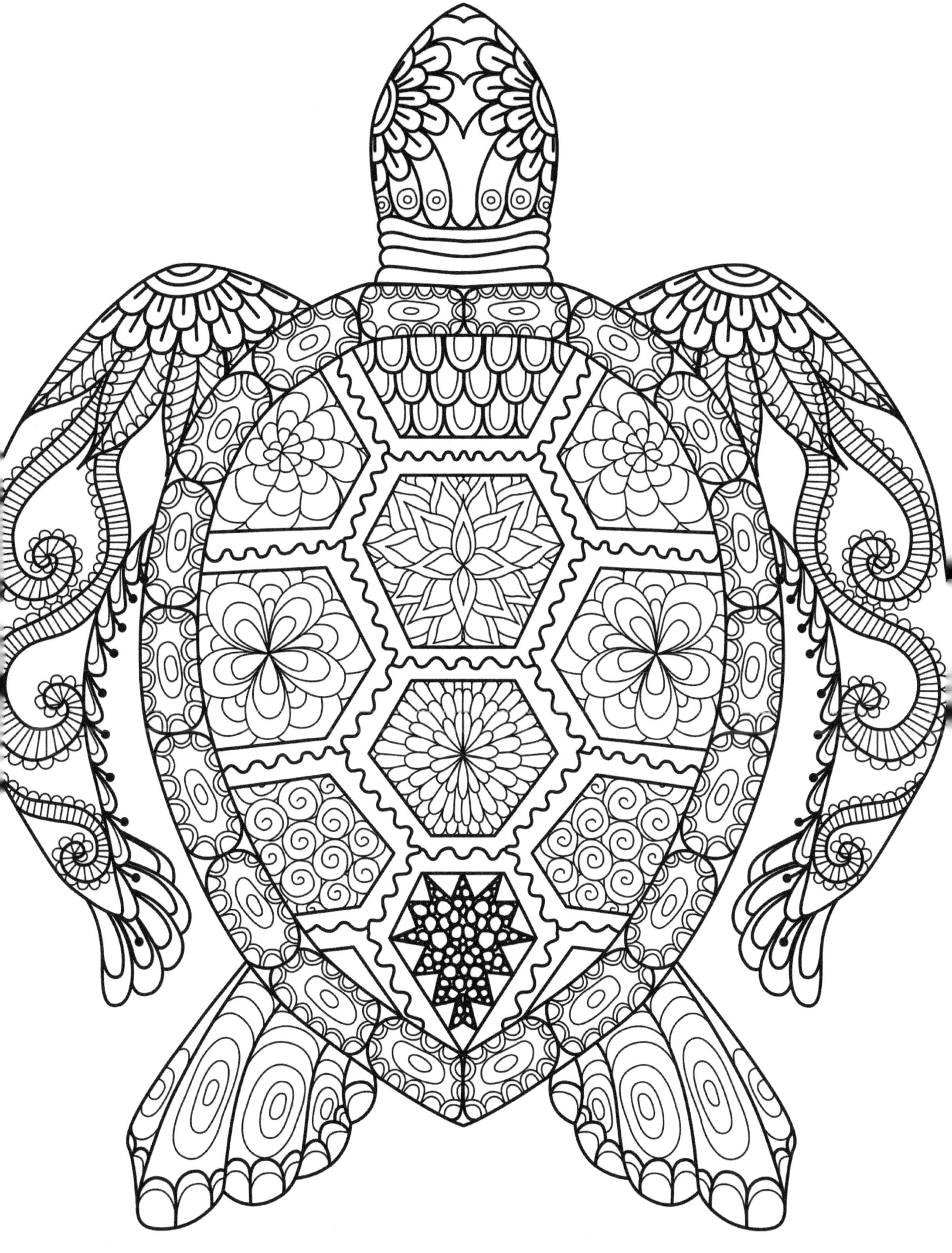

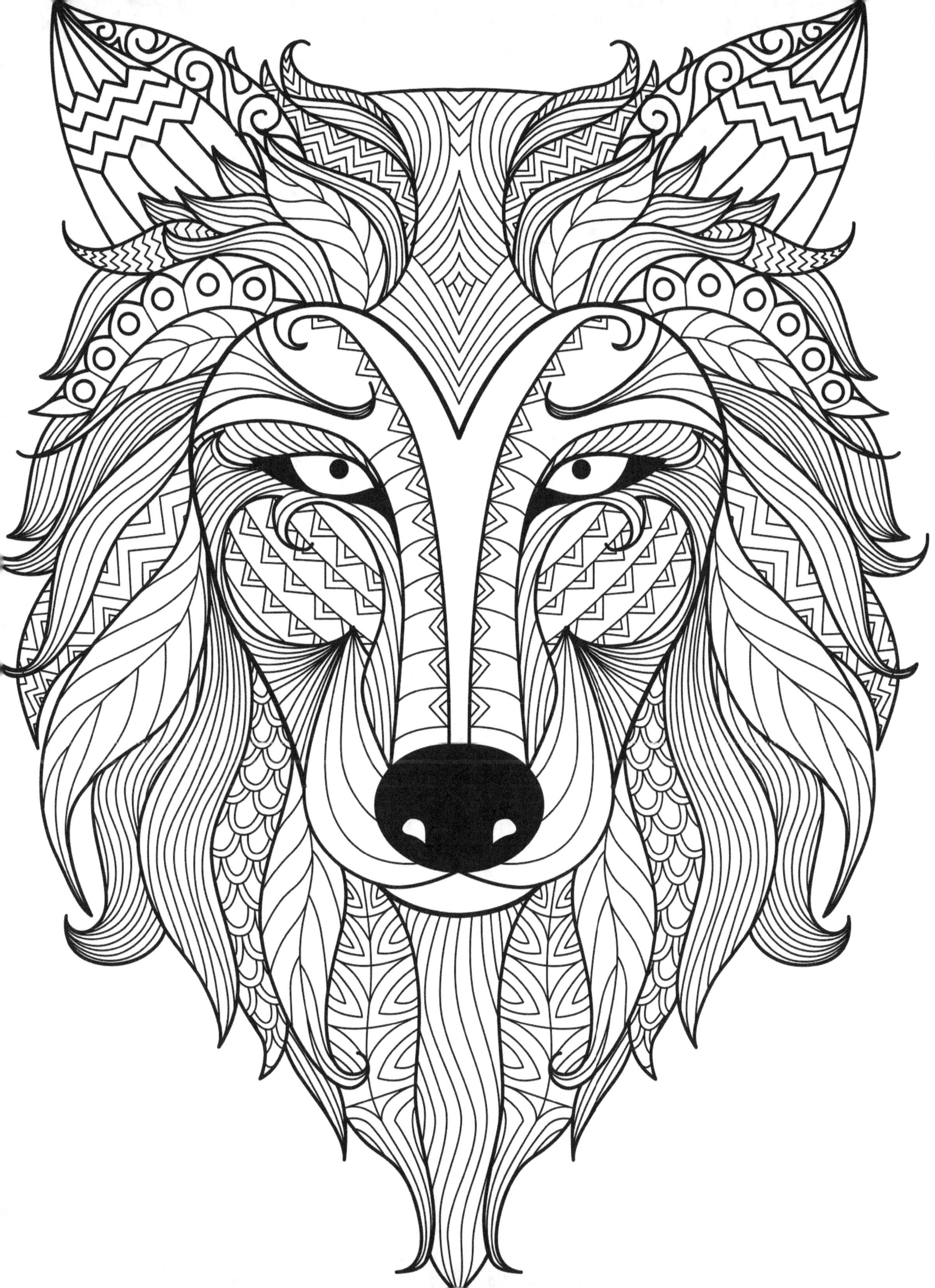

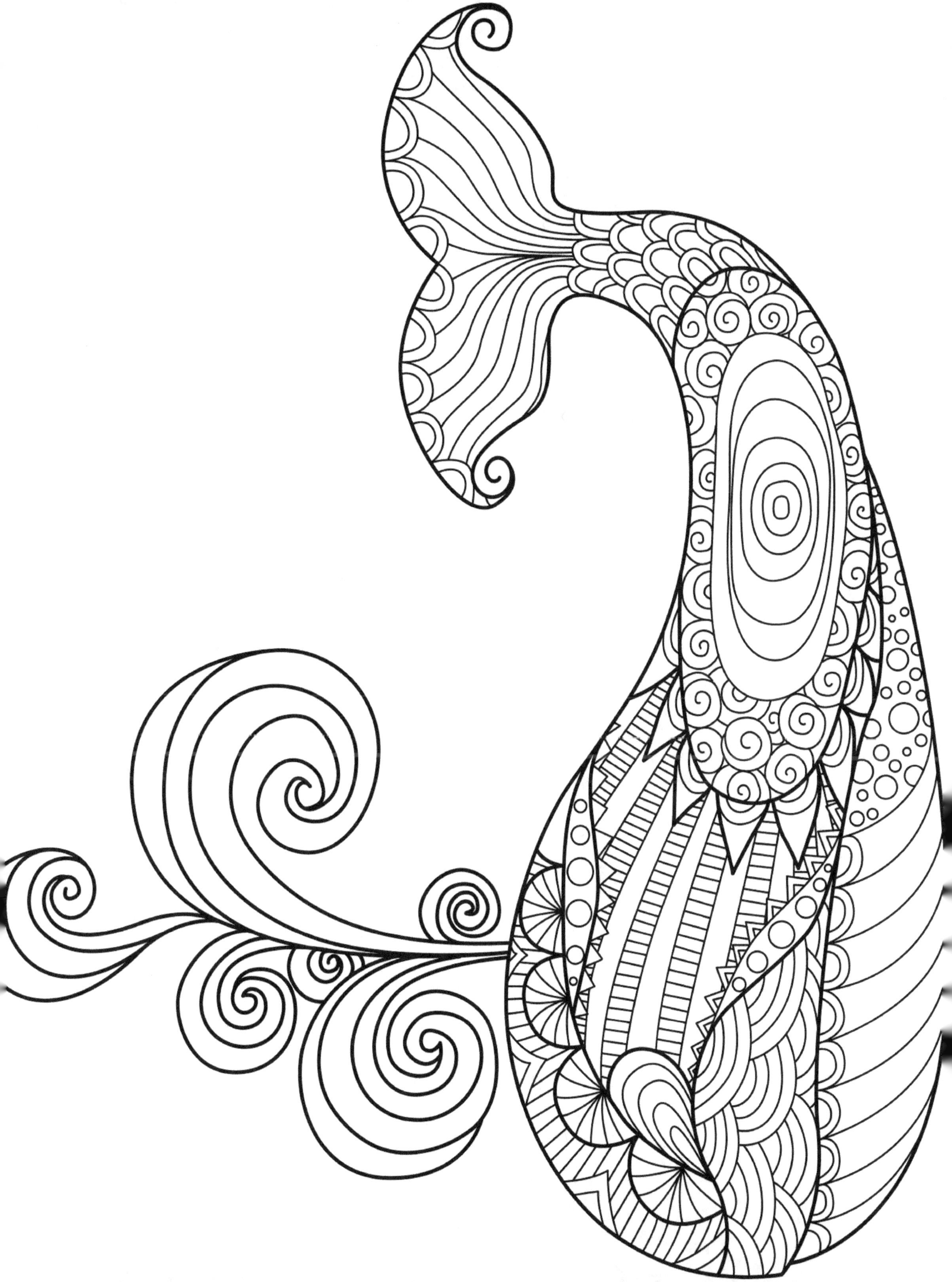

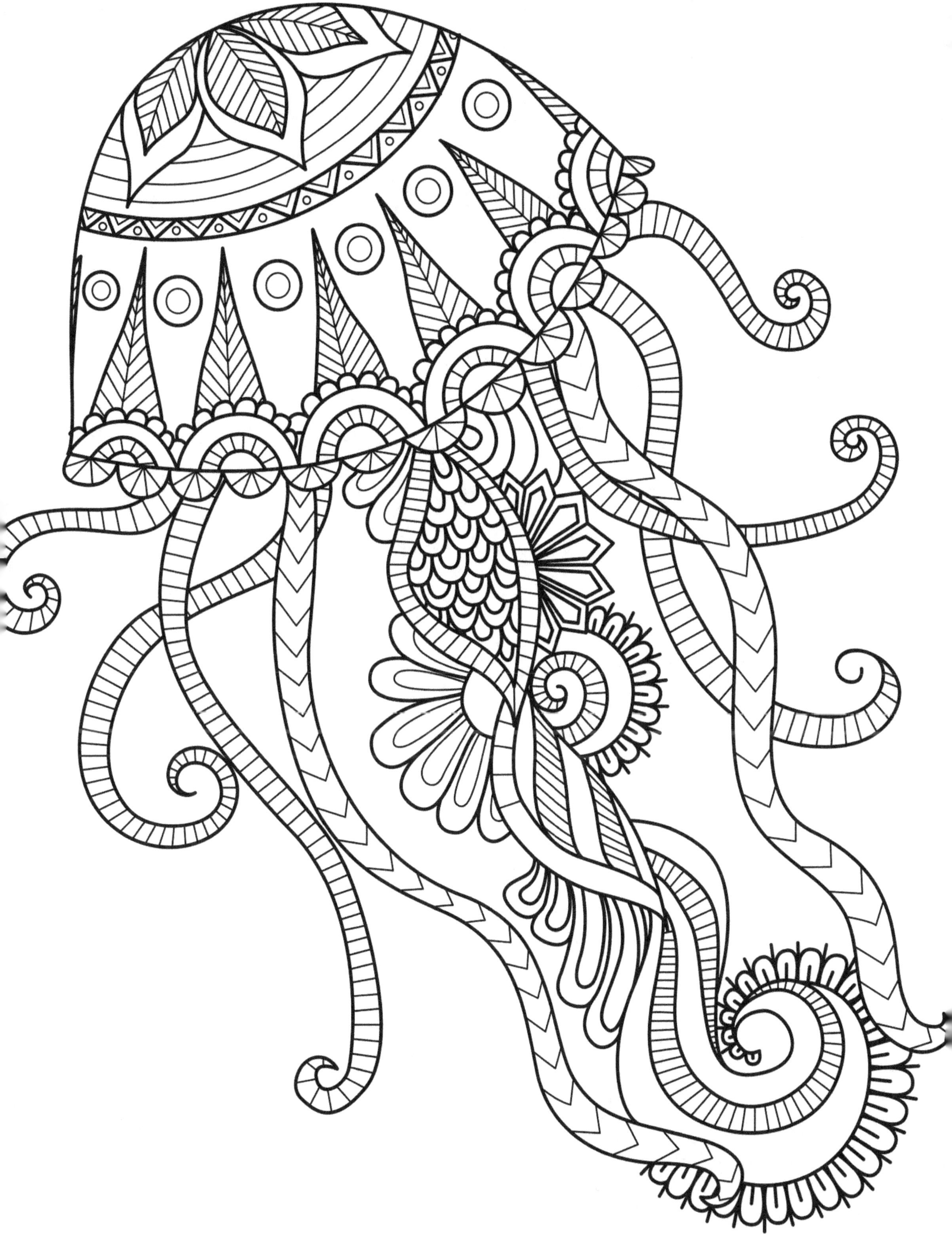

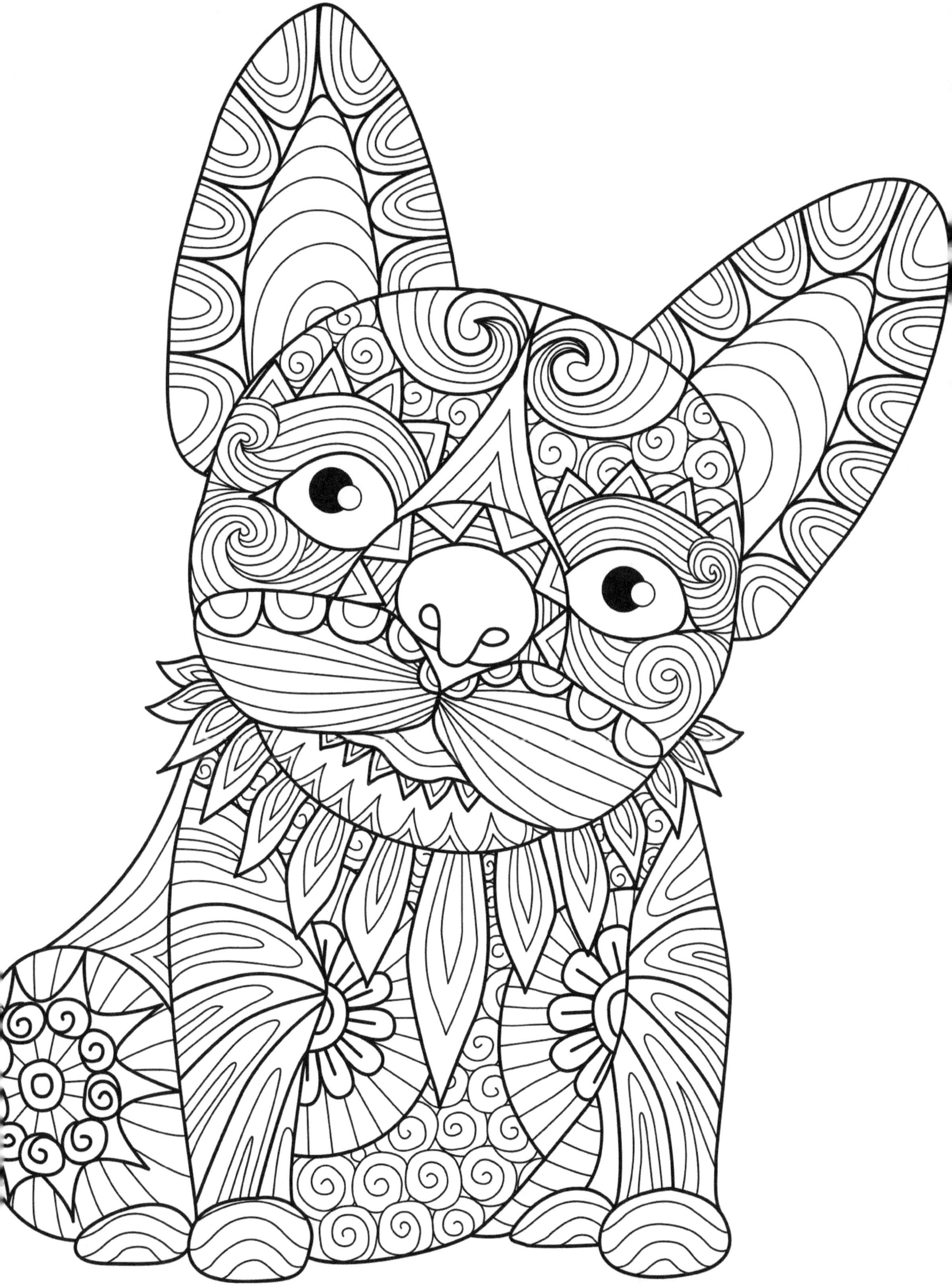

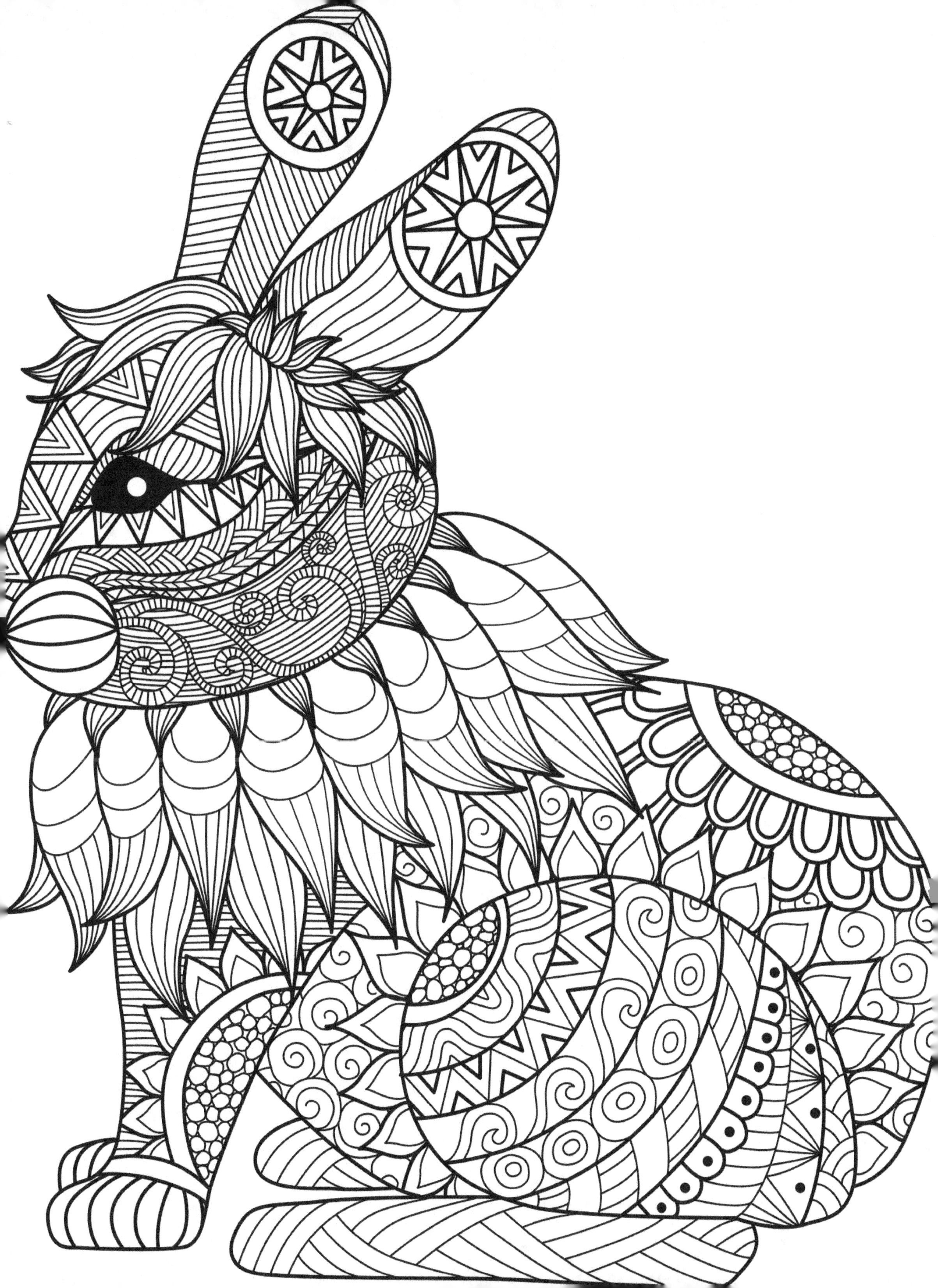

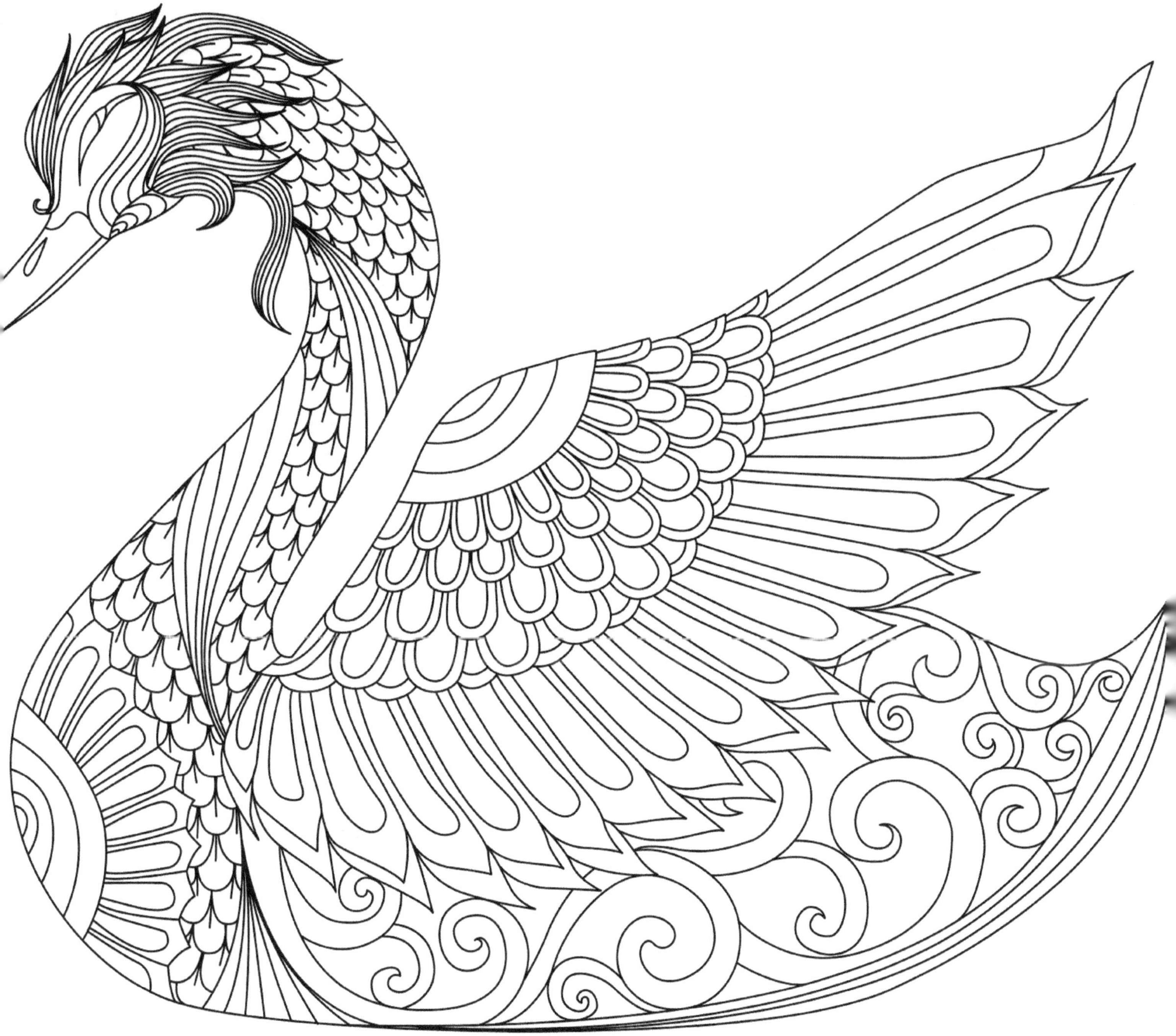

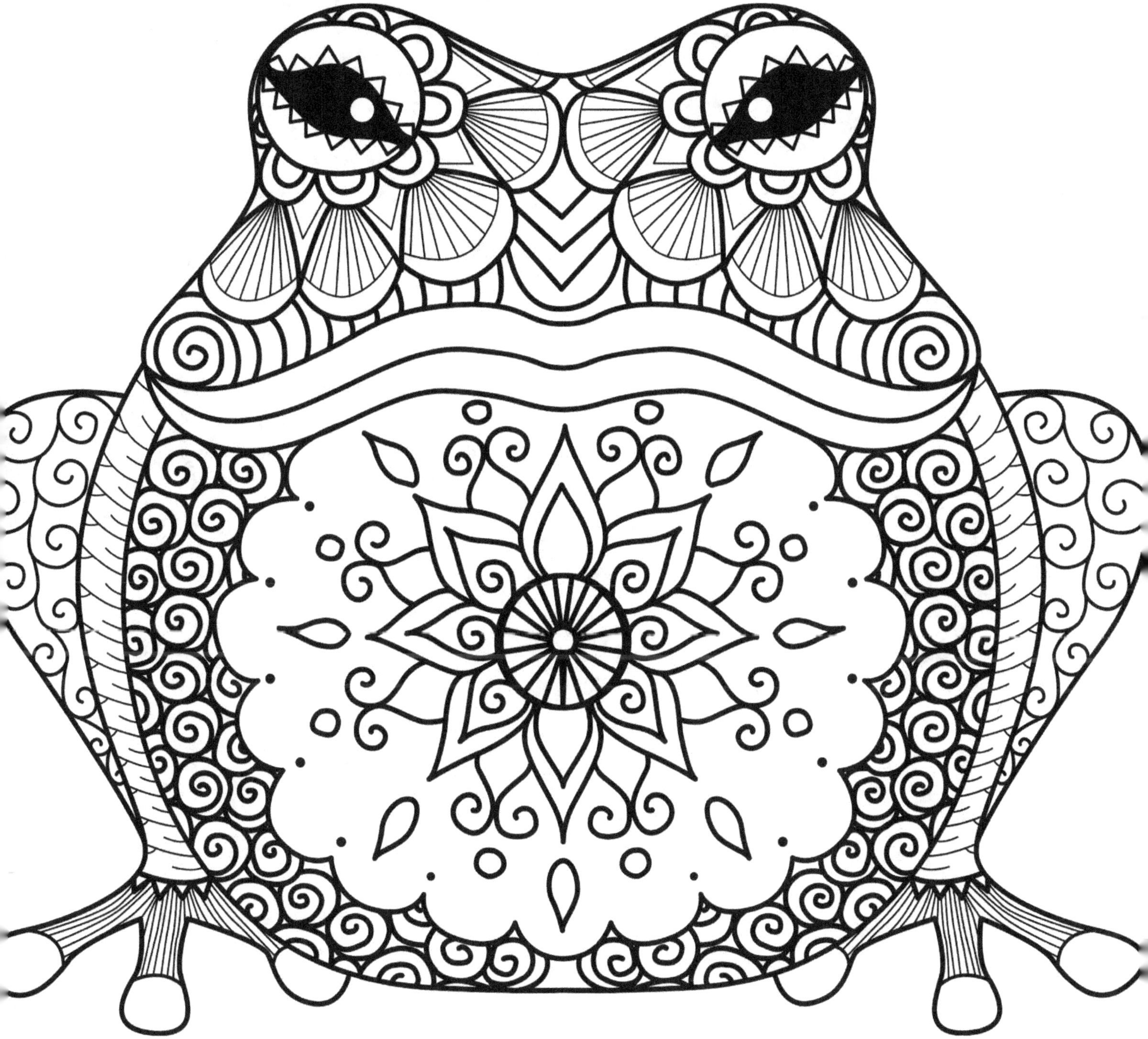

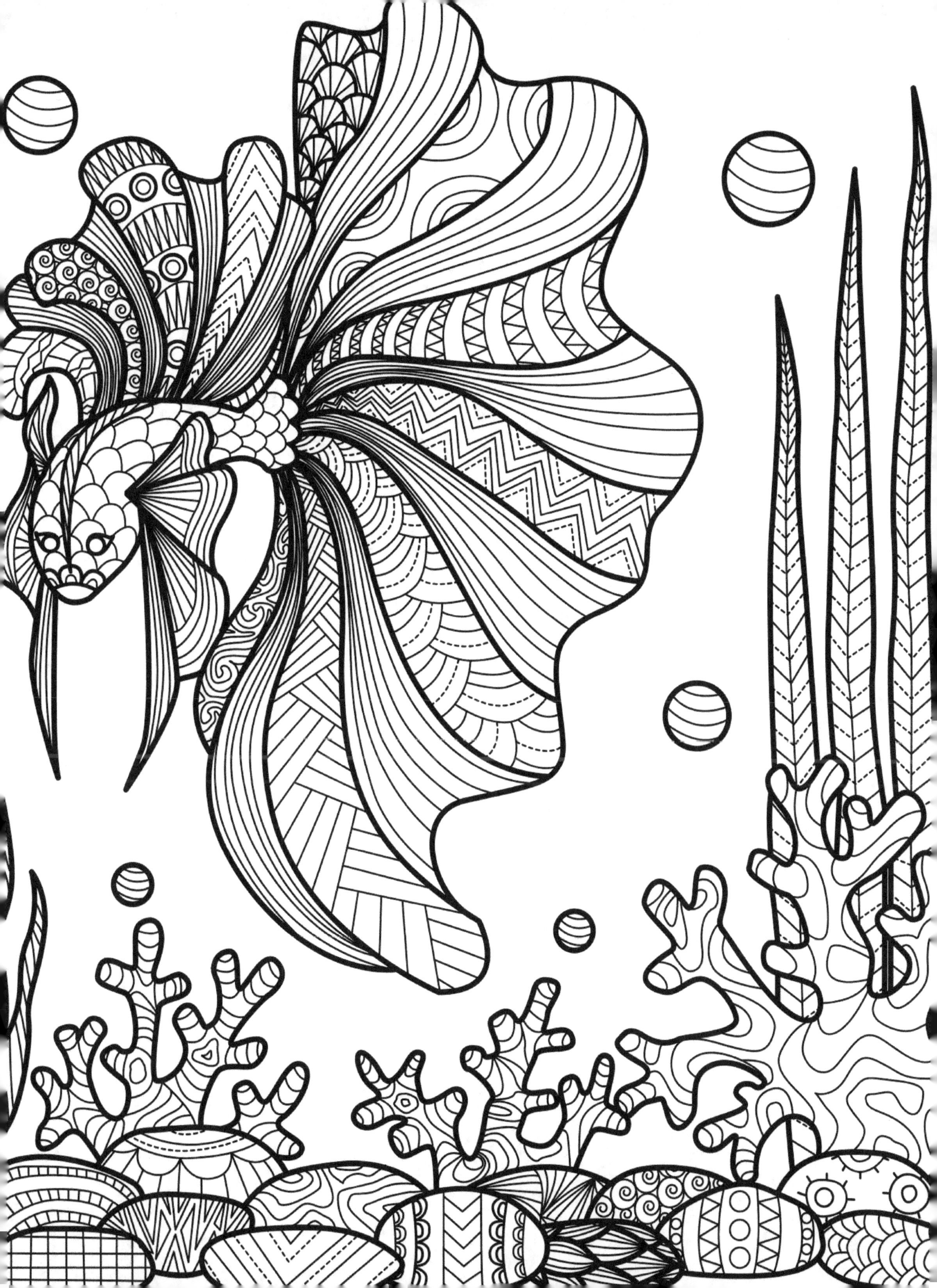

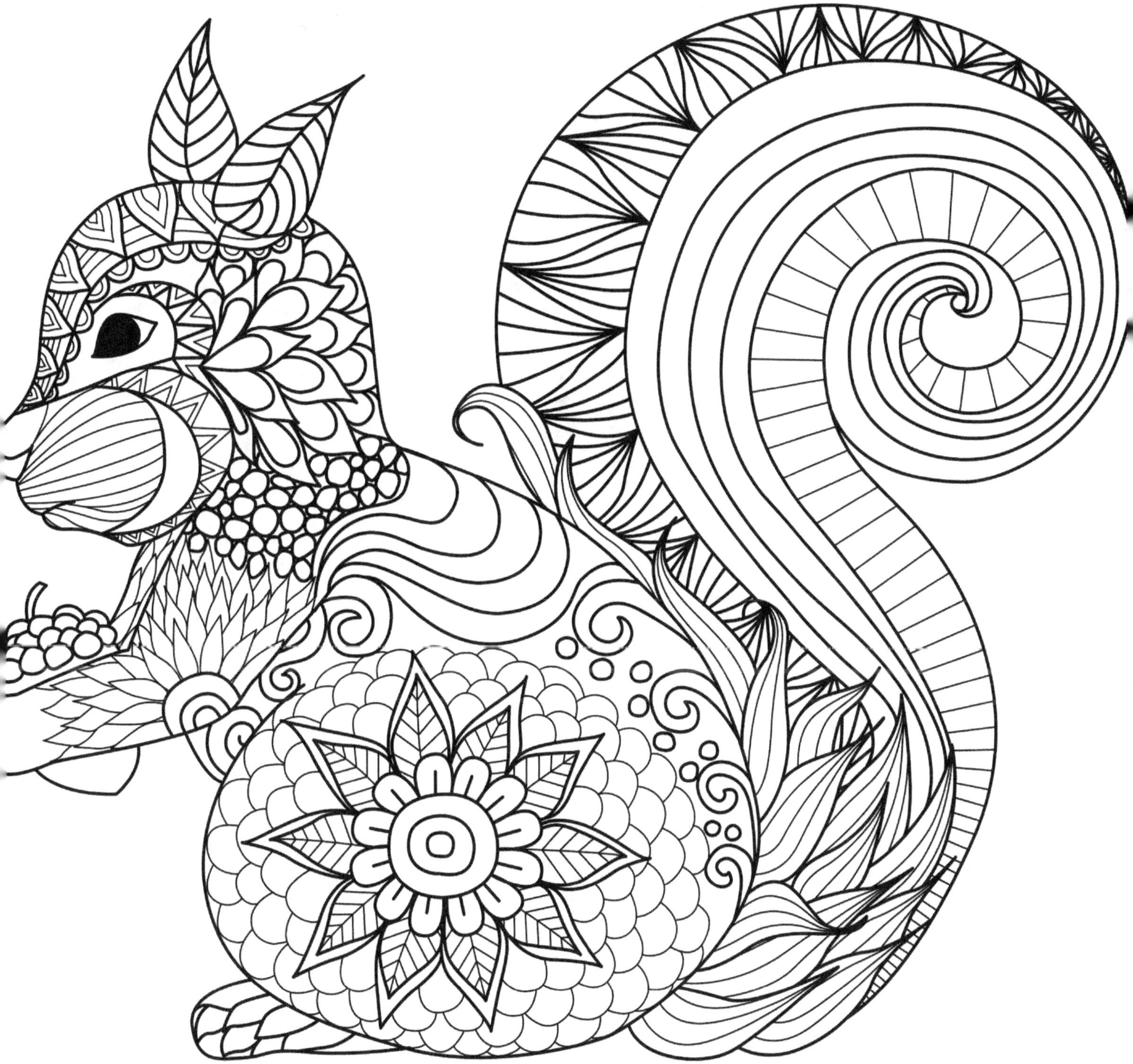

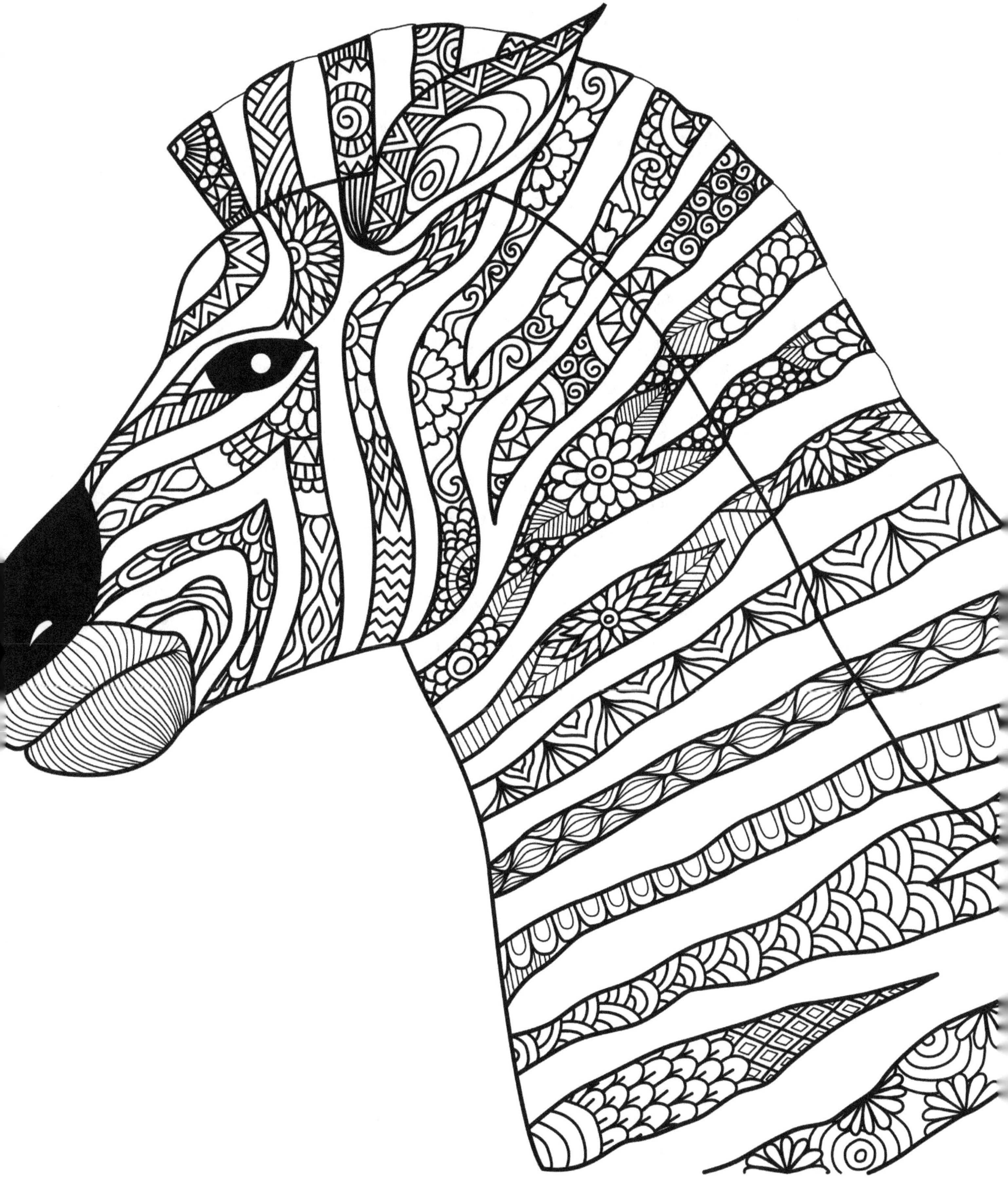

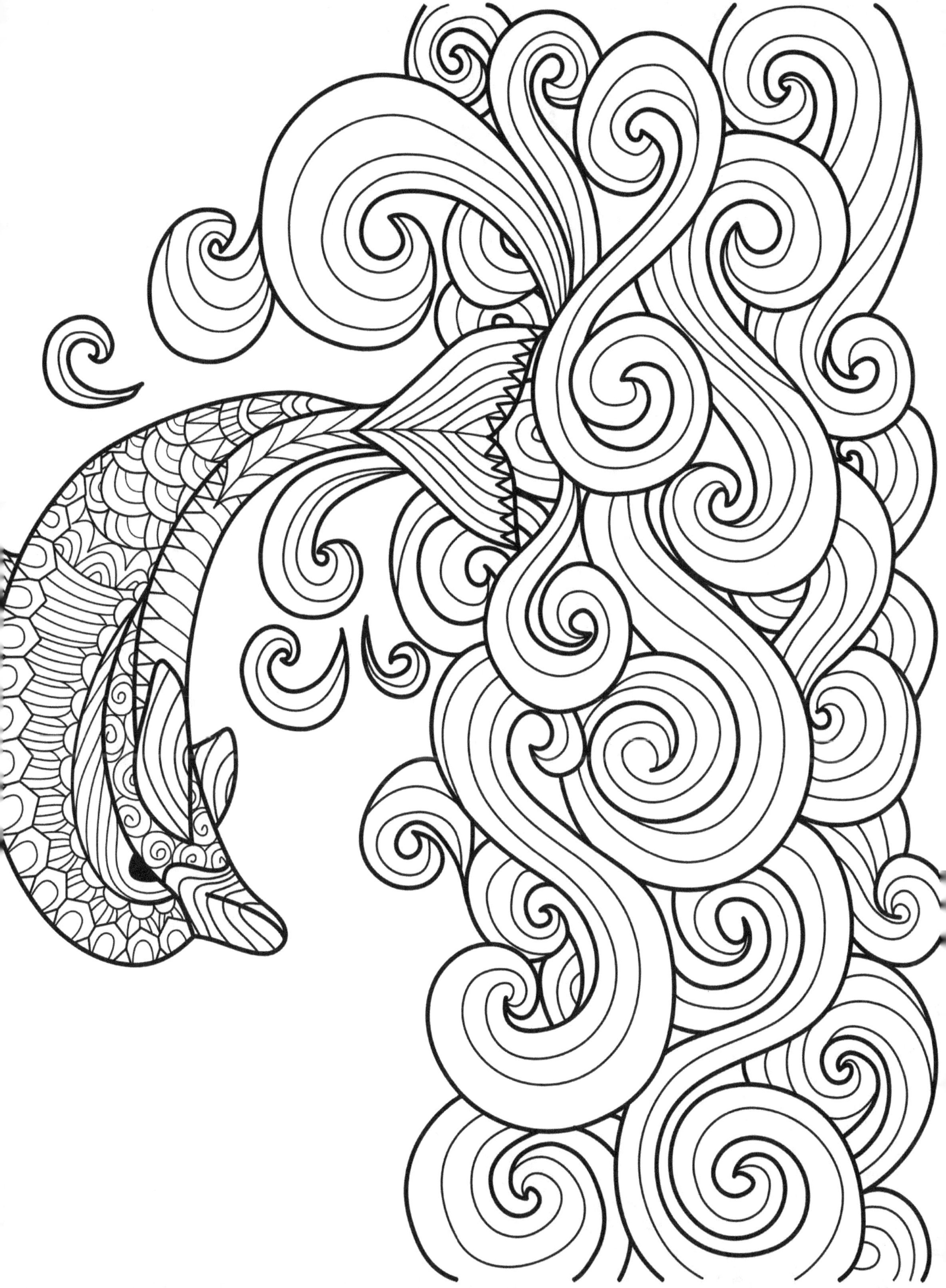

Thank you!

We hope you enjoyed our book!

As a small family company,your feedback is very important to us.

Please let us know what you think about our book at:

G+ adammadison.book@gmail.com

www.ingramcontent.com/pod-product-compliance
Lightning Source LLC
Chambersburg PA
CBHW080855220526
45467CB00008B/2516
9798720999889